RUDOLF STEINER
ON
EDUCATION

A COMPENDIUM BY

ROY WILKINSON

HAWTHORN PRESS

Rudolf Steiner on Education Copyright © 1993 Roy Wilkinson

Published by Hawthorn Press, Hawthorn House,
1 Lansdown Lane, Lansdown, Stroud,
Gloucestershire, GL5 1BJ, United Kingdom
Tel: (01453) 757040 Fax: (01453) 751138
www.hawthornpress.com

Typeset by Glevum Graphics, Gloucestershire

First edition, 1993
Reprinted in 2001 by The Bath Press, Bath

British Library Cataloguing in Publication Data:
Wilkinson, Roy
Rudolf Steiner on Education
I. Title

ISBN 1 869 890 51 5

CONTENTS

RUDOLF STEINER ON EDUCATION

PREFACE

Most of what Rudolf Steiner had to say about education was — literally — said. He gave lecture cycles, courses and single lectures to various people, in various parts of Europe, on many different occasions; some to teachers, some to the general public, some to more intimate circles connected with his work, some to a mixture of all three.

The spoken word demands a different style from that which is written and a lecture is, of necessity, somewhat circumlocutary. In giving lectures on the same subject in different places a certain amount of repetition is inevitable. Furthermore, Rudolf Steiner was Austrian by birth and spoke in German, a language not particularly renowned for brevity of expression. As an honoured guest on many occasions it was necessary for him to preface and to end his discourses with the niceties of polite society. Most of what he said was recorded in shorthand and has been published in book form without the author's revision. Translations have been made into English but they often retain a ponderous style.

For the above reasons the printed works are voluminous and excessive to the reader who requires a reasonably short but comprehensive survey and prefers to read one book instead of twenty. English readers are also more likely to prefer a straightforward English style.

Several writers have attempted to give an overall picture of Rudolf Steiner education, including myself in the book

Commonsense Schooling. When this was first published it was acclaimed in a review in the Times Educational Supplement as, "... a structured and well-written account of Rudolf Steiner education... It translates Steiner's educational thought and methodology into practical English terms. It relates his concept of child development, a beacon amid today's dark gropings, to such matters as classroom practice, school structure, and the need for close correlation between a child's age and the curriculum."

In other words, *Commonsense Schooling* gives an outline of Rudolf Steiner education in a practical sense. The present work attempts something different.

Complaints are often made that Rudolf Steiner's works are long-winded and wordy. This is not surprising when one considers the history of their production. On the other hand, the purists in the Rudolf Steiner fraternity consider that what has been recorded should be treated as Holy Writ and not be tampered with. Those taking this view appear to overlook the facts of origin and development and to realise that what we now have in the published works is quite a distance from the pristine original. I cannot subscribe to the purist outlook but have great sympathy with those who would like to know more of Steiner's views but are put off when confronted with a whole series of books, more or less repetitive.

Ever-growing interest is being shown in Rudolf Steiner's ideas on education and in view of this and the above, it seemed reasonable to provide a compendium of his works on the subject. This book then, *Rudolf Steiner on Education*, is a summary, a condensation, a distillation of what Steiner himself said, omitting repetitions and irrelevances. Obviously the words themselves are not his but I have tried to put his thoughts, without embellishments of my own, except as noted, into acceptable English.

Preface

It has not been an easy task owing to the wealth of material available. Interspersed with lecturing activities, I have spent the best part of four years (of my retirement) poring over the material, analysing, sifting, choosing, discarding and reproducing. It has been a purely personal effort.

The book is not a complete thesis on education. A complete school syllabus was never given. It must also be remembered that on many occasions Dr Steiner was speaking to people familiar with his world conception (Anthroposophy) and therefore some of his statements may appear to be dogmatic, unsubstantiated or aphoristic. Explanations are undoubtedly to be found in other of his works (some 350 volumes covering a great variety of subjects) but it would be beyond the scope of present intent to search out and record every justification for every statement. Such a work would be encyclopaedic.

Allowance must be made for the fact that eighty years have elapsed since the lectures were given. The world has changed. Today's children are different. Technology has advanced. Furthermore, Rudolf Steiner education has been taken up world-wide and what was said in the context of education in Europe may not necessarily hold good in countries with different cultural backgrounds as in the East and native South Africa. Nevertheless what Rudolf Steiner has given in the way of educational ideas is fundamental, even if some of them have to be reviewed, reappraised or updated in the light of changing circumstances and conditions.

From Chapter three onwards this book should be read as if it were reported speech.

Roy Wilkinson, Forest Row, Sussex.

Explanatory note.

Many schools which are conducted on the recommendations of Rudolf Steiner call themselves Waldorf Schools, after the name of the first school of its type. Others simply call themselves Steiner or Rudolf Steiner Schools. Some have a distinctive name and add Waldorf or Rudolf Steiner in some connection as a subtitle. As far as education is concerned, Steiner and Waldorf are used synonymously.

Note on the use of masculine grammatical forms.

The English language has a wonderful vocabulary and provides an extraordinary means of expression. The author however is aware of one particular difficulty and confesses his inability to deal with it. While 'teacher' can refer to either man or woman, a problem arises when it comes to using the pronoun or the possessive adjective. To write he/she or his/hers is clumsy; a continual 'he or she' and 'his or hers' disturbs the flow and so the author follows the usual convention of using the masculine forms which must be taken to include the feminine element. The use of the masculine pronoun, etc., implies no sexual preference.

ONE

A brief sketch of Rudolf Steiner's life and work

From time to time individuals appear on the stage of history whose genius can only be described as universal. Leonardo da Vinci was such a one: painter, sculptor, architect, anatomist, botanist, astronomer, geologist, mathematician, inventor, engineer, writer and philosopher. In the eighteenth century a figure of similar stature was the great poet, scientist and philosopher, Goethe.

From 1861 to 1925 there lived another personality whose accomplishments were even greater than those of Leonardo or Goethe and in whose mind dwelt apparently unbounded earthly and cosmic wisdom. This was Rudolf Steiner.

In England the name is usually associated with education, both for backward and normal children, but from time to time it also occurs in connection with agriculture, medicine, literature and the arts. However, relatively few people have heard it and those who have are a little vague as to its significance.

This is a cause of continual surprise to those who are more familiar with his work since there can have been few men with such gifts in the last century. His achievements are so manifold that they are scarcely credible.

Rudolf Steiner's literary and lecturing output was enormous. The German edition of his collected works (he was Austrian by birth) runs to 350 volumes. In German alone 200,000 of his books are sold annually. Total sales of five fundamental works runs into hundreds of thousands each. Of these *Knowledge of the Higher Worlds; How is it achieved?* and *Theosophy* are the most popular. Pocket editions have topped the million and a half mark.

There are translations of at least some of his works in all European languages as well as in Hebrew, Japanese, Hindi and Turkish. English has the greatest number. There is also an extensive literature produced by his followers.

But writing and lecturing is only one aspect of Rudolf Steiner's work. He was also a practical artist in sculpture and architecture and he created the new art of movement, Eurythmy. His genius was such that he could meet experts on their own ground whatever their speciality. Groups of doctors, teachers, farmers, actors, ministers of religion recognised that here was a man with new ideas and to all these people he gave lectures and advice. The practical result of these meetings has been the foundation of establishments in many countries embodying a new impulse.

In addition to these specialist courses he continued to provide spiritual nourishment and guidance for individuals seeking it. Those personally acquainted with him received some special manna.

Let us take a closer look at this outstanding personality. several biographies of Rudolf Steiner exist and this is not ed to be another. Nevertheless a short resumé of his ork belongs here.

rn in 1861 in what was then Austria-Hungary, ce is situated in what is now Croatia. He died in Dornach, Switzerland in 1925.

In his autobiography he tells us that, as a child, he was aware of the existence of a supersensible world which to him was just as real as the physical, and which was just as full of objects and beings, but he also adds that he felt lonely and cut off from the rest of his fellows because no-one made reference to this 'other' world.

At school and college he studied the official science course (mathematics, chemistry, physics, zoology, botany, geology, mineralogy) but at the same time taught himself the classics. He also took a keen interest in literature and the arts. His degree of Doctor of Philosophy was awarded for a dissertation published later as *Truth and Science*. He worked at the Goethe archives in Weimar and came to appreciate Goethe as a kindred spirit whose view of the world was 'spiritual' like his own.

To call attention to his ideas and to the fact that the time was ripe for a new spiritual impulse, it seemed opportune to accept the editorship of a journal when it was offered. Accordingly he went to Berlin to edit the *Magazin für Litera-tur*, in which were discussed all political, literary, artistic and social problems of the day. At the same time he was pursuing his own studies in order to achieve his doctorate. He also joined the staff of a working men's college and although he was able to expound many of his ideas in these circles, he could only do so within limits.

By the turn of the century he had made a certain position for himself in the world, as a scholar, writer and lecturer. He was nearly forty years old and now felt himself sufficiently mature to speak openly on esoteric matters.

The first opportunity came when he was invited to speak to a group of Theosophists, where he found much sympathy with his views. He was not, however, entirely in accord with

Theosophical thought, particularly in the belief that Christ would reincarnate in a young Indian boy. A number of people who recognised the lecturer's significance decided to found a new society and asked him to be their teacher. Thus the Anthroposophical Society came into existence in 1913. It was reconstituted in 1923 with himself as president.

(It is worth noting that membership of this society is open to all creeds and colours, that it demands no endorsement of doctrine, that the unifying principle is a striving for the knowledge of the Spirit in man and in the universe.)

The necessity for a geographical centre led to the building of the Goetheanum in Dornach, Switzerland.

Dr Steiner's intention was to build a permanent home for Anthroposophical activities, in particular a setting for the performance of his own plays which contain his world conception in the form of drama. Hence it was not to be a mere roof and walls but had to have artistic merit.

As the Egyptians, Greeks, the cathedral-builders of the Middle Ages built their masterpieces out of a spiritual impulse, so the Goetheanum was intended to represent the impulse of the new age. As fate would have it, there were two buildings. The first was a unique and original structure with two intersecting domes, the smaller one over the stage and the larger (bigger than the dome of St Paul's in London) over the auditorium. The interior supporting columns were made of different woods; capitals and bases were carved with different motifs, each one being a metamorphosis of its neighbour. The architraves and window surrounds were also of carved wood. The whole thing was a massive architectural-plastic masterpiece, conceived and designed by Steiner himself. This building, created at enormous cost and by prodigious effort, was destroyed by fire on 31st December 1922, by an act of malice. Its undaunted creator immediately set to work to design a second Goetheanum in a different style, to be built in ferro-concrete, but he did not live to see it completed. This building now stands on the same site as the first one.

With the founding of the Anthroposophical Society and the building of the Goetheanum, Rudolf Steiner's life became one of ceaseless activity — the first Goetheanum, the aftermath of its destruction, lecturing in Dornach, attending to the needs of members — all these made enormous demands on his time and strength. In this connection the tremendous contribution made by his wife should not be overlooked, particularly in the field of artistic activities.

(Marie von Sivers, later Frau Dr Steiner, had been among the audience at a lecture given by Dr Steiner in Berlin in 1902. She belonged to an aristocratic German-Baltic family, grew up in Warsaw, Riga and St Petersburg and had studied the art of speech and recitation in Paris. Her collaboration began almost immediately.)

In addition to the requirements in Dornach, Dr Steiner travelled all over Europe as an exponent of spiritual science. His lectures were by no means theoretical but were also concerned with practical activities such as medicine, agriculture, education. When the Waldorf school was founded in Stuttgart in 1919, he was also very much engaged there.

In the last years of his life he was averaging four hundred engagements annually. He died in March 1925, physically exhausted.

———————

The above is an outline of his life but we still have to clarify the special feature, the essence — so to speak — of Rudolf Steiner.

To say that the world is beset with problems, that the social order is rapidly deteriorating and that crises abound in all spheres of human activity is merely to repeat platitudes. To say that Rudolf Steiner has solutions may sound sufficiently presumptuous to make the reader drop this book immediately. Perhaps it would be better to say that Rudolf Steiner has proposals which would bring about solutions but that they need open minds, understanding hearts and willing hands.

In view of the enormous strides in technology many people today view the future with some apprehension, but Rudolf Steiner was calling attention to such dangers in the first years of this century. He also offered positive antidotes.

The problems, however, are not only outward. They exist in the inner being of man, although ultimately they may be identical.

When the human being comes to a consciousness of himself, questions arise as to his own being, his nature, his destiny. In an age which has lost both insight and faith and has become purely materialistic, the answers are difficult to find and problems remain unsolved in the soul — hence a possible cause for the malaise in society today.

Rudolf Steiner realised that the natural-scientific age and its consequences would bring about the downfall of mankind unless counterbalanced by some other influence. He felt it his mission to point this out and to bring some counter-impulse. He considered that the turn of the century, 1900, was a vital point. He was not alone in this. Many other thinkers had the same view and their number has increased with the passing years but there is a difference between what the founder of Anthroposophy advocates and what is put forward by conventional reformers. The latter see salvation in democracy, universal education, social planning, belief possibly in divine intervention, a return to past moral values. It is a patching of the old ship. Steiner requires a new one. To be specific — he considered that the time was ripe for the knowledge of the spiritual world, the Kingdom of God, to be made public and that it should be possible for all people to attain it directly (eventually) by personal effort, an effort which has ethical implications.

It is obvious that Rudolf Steiner's own gifts were exceptional. He had the faculty of entering a world which is closed to most of us and this he could do in full consciousness. He had spiritual vision, extended consciousness — call it what you will. He claimed to speak only of his own experiences and to give the results of his own investigations. From his spiritual insight this 'spiritual' scientist was able to offer knowledge, guidance and a new impulse. It must be emphasised that his way has nothing to do with so-called spiritualism or mediumship, whereby certain experiences may be obtained by a dampening down of the consciousness or where there is a phenomenon of knocks, voices or materialisations. The distinctive factor is his clear, fully conscious method of development and investigation and the manner in which the facts are recorded and related to physical phenomena. For anyone who takes the trouble to study it, the synthesis of his whole work confirms its truth.

He saw it as his mission to bring spiritual knowledge to earthly understanding, to give scientific explanations which justify the claims of religion, and to create a bridge between the physical and the spiritual world.

The new development he called Anthroposophy.

———————

There can be no simple answer to the question: What is Anthroposophy? If we had a word like Weltanschauung, as in

German, we might describe it as such. The nearest we can get in English is 'conception of the world' but this sounds dry and academic. Perhaps we should first dispel a few illusions and say what it is not. It is not a system, nor a collection of theories, nor a cult, doctrine or dogma, code or sect. It is too universal.

According to the scholars, the word itself is composed of Anthropos, meaning man, and Sophia, meaning wisdom or knowledge. But the derivation of Anthropos is of some significance. It is a word which means 'turning upwards'. An Anthropos therefore is a man who looks up into the heights. Thus the sense of the word Anthroposophy would be 'wisdom of knowledge of man who considers the source of his life to be in the heights'; i.e. knowledge of the spiritual as well as of the physical man.

Rudolf Steiner uses the word as synonymous with spiritual science. Why should he use the word 'Anthropos' (man)? It could be argued that spiritual science is divine wisdom, i.e. 'Theos' (God). Man is however of divine creation. He is one with the world. "Man", says Steiner, "is the answer to the world riddle." Hence Anthroposophy is a body of knowledge concerning the spiritual in man and in the universe.

The wisdom-filled natural world is a wonderful place, but knowledge of the sense-world alone does not give an answer to the riddles of existence. The human being knows this instinctively and hence the need for knowledge of the spirit arises as a need of the human soul. The material world as apprehended by our senses requires a spiritual interpretation to become intelligible.

Such knowledge is perhaps even more urgent in our present age to balance the all-pervading effect of materialistic thinking. A healthy strengthening of inner activity counteracts the exhausting effects of outer life. If a firm foundation for morality is required, the soul must have knowledge and truth. The information provided by Anthroposophy gives food for thought and meditation. But there is a stage beyond this. Conscious inner activity develops new organs of perception.

Thus Anthroposophy provides a path to the attainment of direct knowledge of higher worlds.

At first sight it might seem remote that something connected with spiritual matters, with soul development, dealing with questions of eternity, should be practical. We should remember however that originally all activities were directed out of a spiritual impulse, first by spiritual leaders who received their inspiration directly, but which, in the course of time, became tradition. In Anthroposophy is a new revelation. Anthroposophical ideas have given rise to fruitful developments in many spheres of activity.

In this sense it could be said that Anthroposophy is a practical science.

More detailed information will be found in the third chapter of this book, *The necessity for spiritual insight.*

TWO

Rudolf Steiner's educational work

Occupying an important place in the developments arising out of Anthroposophy is the new educational movement. It has an interesting history, centred obviously around the personality of its founder who was a teacher in one form or another for most of his life.

In the normally accepted sense, Rudolf Steiner became a teacher in his early youth. His parents were poor but he was a gifted scholar and soon turned his talents to earning money to pay for his own further schooling. Already at the age of fourteen he was giving private tuition. Later, as a student, he supported himself entirely in this way. It meant that he had to study subjects which were not in his particular course in order to teach others. Since his pupils were often of the slow-learner type, he had to reconstruct and adapt his lessons to meet their special needs. This also gave him great insight into the workings of the mind.

He had a rewarding and special experience when he was asked to educate an abnormal child, a hydrocephalic, who was considered unteachable. This task lasted several years but in time the boy was able to attend the state school where he successfully passed his examinations and in due course became a doctor.

In his autobiography, Rudolf Steiner acknowledges the value of these years of tutoring for his own later educational work.

As a person interested in all facets of human existence, he naturally had ideas about education and schools. In 1884 he had already expressed his opinion that they should be free from governmental control. He voiced his ideas in lectures given in various capitals of Europe and the essence of what he had to say was then published in 1907 in the booklet *Education of the Child from the Standpoint of Spiritual Science*. However, his public work in education did not start until much later.

The impulse for this came from outside. It came at the end of the first World War, at a time of utter despair in central Europe.

Dr Steiner was concerned that there should be some positive reconstruction of the social order and in various writings and lectures he had enunciated his ideas for a renewal based on his understanding of the threefold nature of man which should be reflected in society. He advocated a re-orientation of the whole social order by a division of responsibilities into three spheres. These are the spiritual, the economic and the sphere of rights. They are an echo of what had been proclaimed in the French revolution but not carried through at the time, Liberty, Equality, Fraternity: liberty in the spiritual sphere, equality in the sphere of rights, fraternity in that of economics. Although these ideas created some interest among important politicians and people in government circles in central Europe in 1919, they were not adopted. Nevertheless they were embraced by other groups of people who saw in them hope for the future.

Among the persons interested was the director of the Waldorf-Astoria cigarette factory in Stuttgart, an enlightened employer, Emil Molt. He had come to the view that at the heart of the recent catastrophe lay a faulty and neglected way of education. He recognised that education belongs to the spiritual sphere and should be free from any domination by outside authority, be it political or economic. There must be freedom for the teacher and a setting-free of the capacities of pupils. Then minds would be open and with more emphasis on culture there would be less unrest and feeling of frustration. With greater knowledge and insight there would be less likelihood of running into blind alleys and further calamities.

Molt had already organised educational courses for his workers. Now he decided to found a school for their children and he asked Dr Steiner to prepare the ground and become the director.

The offer was accepted and work began. Teachers were chosen, trained, inspired and appointed. They did not necessarily have an academic background and came from the most varied walks of life. It is doubtful if ever such a brilliant group of educators had come together before or if such has ever occurred since.

On 7th September 1919 the Waldorf school opened its doors. It was intended for the children of the factory workers but soon friends and others came along wishing to enrol their children. They came from every class of society. Within a few years there were over a thousand children and seventy-six teachers. For lack of space many children had to be turned away.

Interest in the school spread. Dr Steiner was invited to give lectures and courses on education all over Europe, but in his lifetime only three other schools were founded. (He died in 1925.) Subsequently the schools grew and flourished. Under the Hitler regime they received a set-back in Germany and the occupied territories, where they were closed on the admitted grounds of encouraging individualism, which was inimical to the state. At the end of the war they re-opened under great difficulties but with great enthusiasm. Elsewhere there has been continuous development and there are now approaching six hundred such schools world wide including one each in Israel, Egypt, India and Japan. Some schools have adopted the name Waldorf; some take a name, e.g. The .... Rudolf Steiner School; some have an individual appellation. As far as education is concerned, Waldorf and Rudolf Steiner are synonymous.

It must be pointed out that it was never the intention to found 'private' schools but, owing to circumstances, this is the way in which most of them have to function. It was hoped that the new ideas and inspiration would flow into the general educational field.

Mention must also be made of the many homes and schools which now exist in the field of curative education.

To avoid any misapprehension, let it be stated clearly that the Waldorf or Rudolf Steiner schools do not teach Anthroposophy. This is the background out of which the curriculum, method of presentation and the attitude of the teachers are formed.

It is an interesting fact that many of the most important lecture cycles on education were given in England.

THREE

The necessity for spiritual insight

One of the subjects most hotly debated at the present time is that of education. It is felt that what is offered in our schools is unsatisfactory and, judging by the proliferation of problems in society, so are its products. Too many people have problems in not knowing what to do with their lives, and education — or lack of it — must bear its share of the blame.

There are many caring and clever people who have ideas as to what should be done and optimistically set up programmes of educational reform. Some of these deal purely with externalities, but many express ideals which in themselves are to be commended although sometimes coloured by religious, political or social ideas. However, they all suffer from the fact that they do not touch the core of the problem. They remain abstractions because they are not founded on a true understanding of the human being. The same could be said of instruction in the teacher training colleges. Evidence shows that when teachers have to face a class of children they feel at a loss and the question must pose itself as to why. Could it be that they have not been taught about the essential nature of man?

Education is the most important problem of the present time. Our whole future depends on it. The present social system is on the verge of collapse, yet the education system grinds on in a more-or-less set pattern, with a little tinkering here and there.

What has to be realised is that instruction and education are not synonymous. Education means development. Proper education means development of the whole human being. Instruction, the teaching of subjects, is a means to this end, not an end in itself. We need an education which makes us not only clever and intelligent but also sensible, and one which also creates enthusiasm and inner mobility and provides nourishment for the soul.

The reason for the failure in education and the reason why teachers fail to cope is a lack of the right sort of knowledge. Psychologies and manuals of instruction exist in abundance but they miss the point. A real education can only be provided on the basis of a real knowledge of man, a knowledge which embraces the whole human being, body, soul and spirit. Then the right nourishment will be given at the right age and the right forces awakened in the requisite periods of early life.

We live in a materialistic age. The education provided reflects the modern materialistic intellectual outlook. Today we have very advanced natural science and various religious denominations which purport to represent spiritual life. Natural science tells us a great deal about the human being but does not look into his essential nature. We should ask ourselves what sort of an idea of human value does science give? Does it give satisfactory answers with regard to man's origin, his purpose in life, his inner nature? Does it likewise give a satisfactory answer regarding the question of creation and evolution of the world? Scientific explanations, however elaborate and apparently logical, do not satisfy the inner longings of the soul. Today's conceptions of world origin are hypothetical because we have lost contact with the spiritual. The same can be said about the nature of man.

A true understanding of man cannot come from the sort of thinking which designates the heart a pump and gives the idea of the human being as a superior technical, mechanical contraption. Under the influence of this same thinking ideals become illusions, the spiritual life is a phantom and only economic progress is real. We have been led to believe that there can only be positive knowledge of those things which the senses observe and the intellect acquires through sense observation. We have lost sight of creation as a deed of the gods and we have lost sight of the human being as the highest creation upon earth of divine spiritual powers.

One might imagine that some understanding of these matters might be forthcoming in the field of religion, but there we find confusion, even ignorance. In the religious sphere we find beliefs which give a certain amount of comfort to the faithful, but which are in conflict with the findings of science. Faith and belief, however, are not sufficient for the modern mind, which wants to *know*.

There is basically no conflict between religion and science. What is required is more knowledge.

The point of view put forward here is that natural science gives us knowledge of material things but that the world and the human being are an expression of spiritual forces and hence what is needed is a complementary 'spiritual science'. (The word 'spiritual' used here should not be confused with so-called spiritualism, spiritism, or other mystical, fanatical, superstitious sects or movements. It is a general term for the non-material, the supersensible.)

Spiritual science is nothing new, but the form of its manifestation changes. In former ages, men were aware of supersensible worlds. They had direct contact with the beings of these worlds and received guidance and inspiration from them. Through practice of Yoga or asceticism, spiritual insight was attainable. In the course of history the faculty faded as far as the general mass of mankind was concerned, but it was retained or attained by certain personalities through a process known as initiation. In Egypto-Chaldaic times the initiates could still unite themselves with the spiritual powers of the cosmos; in Greece the ability faded and the new power of thinking evolved — hence the beginning of philosophy.

When man had direct experience of spiritual beings, he felt himself within the divine creative power and this was his inspiration which was brought to expression in art and ritual. At the same time it was the source of knowledge (science) and morality.

In our modern age spiritual vision has been lost and the former disciplines for obtaining it are no longer applicable. The thinking which has replaced it has concentrated on the material world and hence the enormous discoveries of natural science and their application. It is, however, through further activating this very power of thinking that the way opens today to higher knowledge, but it must be accompanied by moral development. There is nothing strange or mystical in this. It is not a matter of acquiring great knowledge but of training the mind. Concentration and memory exercises, together with the cultivation of moral attitudes, develop soul forces so that eventually a higher consciousness is attained. One becomes aware of spiritual beings, of the spiritual forces manifesting in matter, of the eternal nature of the human spirit. These could be called religious experiences. Belief becomes knowledge.

Although all may strive and aspire, it is not everyone who will become an initiate, but what the initiates bring to light is accessible to every healthy understanding. Those who do not possess the faculty need only consider the revelations of those who do, and use their reason and unprejudiced observation to test their correctness and value. The knowledge which thus becomes available is what is termed here spiritual science.

Spiritual science can be studied with great profit for its own sake, but it has very definite practical applications of which education is one. It gives knowledge of the whole human being and such knowledge is vital to the provision of a proper education. In theological terms, one could say that to study spiritual science is to acknowledge God; to educate is to recognise and further the divine intentions.

In seeking to acquire a knowledge of man the educationalist should also be aware of the changing nature of the human being, not only within the limits of his own experience but also in evolution. Even today's child is different from the one of yesteryear and the nature of man has undergone vast changes in the course of a few thousand years. Observing both the small and large changes will give the right perspective for teaching and so provide the right approach for the present generation. Any teacher with at least twenty years experience will perceive the smaller changes in the course of his or her own career; to appreciate the larger ones it is necessary to cast a glance over past history.

What were the ideals of education in the past? And how were they related to the humanity of the particular age?

The history of civilisation shows not only that direct spiritual vision has faded in favour of sense perception and thinking, but that group consciousness under a leader has given way to individual consciousness and decision.

In ancient civilisations one could not think of an education based on teaching. It was based on a relationship between the initiate and the disciple, the Guru and the Chela, and it was a matter of example and imitation.

Greek education was based on gymnastics, human movement. It was the continuation of an ideal of earlier civilisations which had practised Yoga. In Greek culture care was taken that the pupil should learn how to move, how to bear heat and cold, how to adapt to the physical world. There was a feeling that the soul-spiritual nature of man developed rightly in a rightly developed physical body. In harmonious movement the Greek was inspired and felt spiritual and soul forces flowing through him. Bodily training brought about a co-ordinated way of thinking — hence it was the basis for the study of mathematics, philosophy, music, geometry, etc., and for developing memory and habits.

To some extent the Romans copied the Greek pattern but there was a change from cultivating the whole physical body to cultivating only the middle region, that is, the rhythmic system. Speech was the means. The Romans expected that through the use of plastically, picturesquely formed speech, they would affect body and spirit. There was no intellectual learning as such and the Rhetorician took the place of the Gymnast as educator. This was continued into the Middle Ages, in the monastic schools. The training was essentially one of soul forces. The Rhetorician was one who could do something with his powers of soul, namely, convince through speech. But spiritual knowledge was now encapsulated in tradition and it became more and more necessary to train the memory. Knowledge based on tradition became faith.

Since the 15th Century, 'head' culture has developed. The ideal was to be erudite, to know. In the course of history spiritual vision disappeared; the idea of a spiritual world receded; material things became of the greatest importance. Sense perception is the decisive factor and hence the desire to educate only by means of sense perception. The educator is the savant, the professor. He imparts information. General development is neglected in favour of the acquisition of knowledge. Pupils must become 'learned'. The Grammar Schools are a relic of this attitude.

Now there is a new impulse in the world. It is felt that education should involve the development of the whole human being. The 'professor' principle should be superseded.

In the past, education was only for the select few. Today, with the feeling of individuality, ego-consciousness, an experience of inner freedom, education must be for every human being and, in view of world-wide consciousness, it must contain worldwide, even cosmic perspectives. The modern age demands education for all, not men and women who belong to a particular class, nation or professional category. Each individual human being is entitled to an education which will develop his or her own inherent qualities and, at the same time, be an introduction to the world at large. It follows that the principles of education must be free from all distinctions of class, sex or creed and be free from outside influence. Today life demands all-round vision. The enquiring mind seeks to acquire knowledge but a knowledge that also satisfies the soul.

The teacher is working towards the future. He has to develop wholeness within himself and relate to the child — something which he can only achieve by acquiring a proper knowledge of living human nature. He is not called upon to teach the world outlook which spiritual science gives, but he can allow it to inspire him and fructify his own thinking and then maybe he will not clog children's minds with dross which hinders their future enlightenment.

What is it then that spiritual science has to offer?

Spiritual science explains how supersensible forces are at work in nature and in the cosmos. It provides an explanation of world evolution which satisfies the demands of science and religion.

It gives knowledge of man, of his divine origin and of the essential being behind the exterior form.

It deals with questions of existence before birth and after death, together with those of karma and destiny. It points to the individual's involvement with the whole of the rest of mankind and the universe and brings him to realise that his own acts have a cosmic, universal significance.

It shows how supersensible forces work in the bodily organisation and how, particularly in childhood, they manifest at different ages.

It looks at life as a whole in the realisation that influences in youth have their effect throughout life, even to the extent that wrong educational practices lead to physical illnesses in later life.

It analyses the temperaments of children and explains how to deal with them. It points to the effect of the teacher's temperament on his pupils.

It relates the manner of teaching and choice of subjects to chronological age.

In the light of human development it points to the tasks of education at the present time.

Education is a social matter. Society, the social organisation, is a reflection of the human being. If social conditions are to improve, a start must be made with an improvement in the attitudes and work of individuals. This means an appropriate education and people with insight and will to carry it out. Thus spiritual science has a contribution to make towards solving social problems.

In general, the study of spiritual science stimulates and awakens the mind. It provides inspiration in artistic, moral and religious spheres as well as practical ones. In education the practice of its recommendations for self-improvement enhance the capacity of the teacher and further his own development. It induces responsibility.

With sufficient knowledge of the human being, a solution to educational problems can be found. It is one of the aims of spiritual science to provide this knowledge.

FOUR

The being of man

"So God created man in his own image, in the image of God created he him. Male and female created he them."

There will be general agreement that education should be founded on the knowledge of man but if we accept the divine origin of the human being, then it is obvious that material science cannot give us a true picture of him. Spiritual science must come to our aid and the information that spiritual science can give is endless. This being the case, what is given here cannot be considered as more than an outline.

The Cosmic and Eternal Man

We will first put forward a view of man in the setting of the cosmos and eternity. Such a view cannot be acquired once and for all. It needs to be continually processed in the mind and expanded. Objections will certainly be raised to these 'fancy' ideas, but anyone who cares to study them sufficiently and objectively will soon be convinced of their validity.

The human being, built up by the forces of the cosmos and sustained by them, is the highest creation of divine powers. In his physical structure he has the impress of the Zodiac; in his organs the planets. He is related to all things in earth and heaven — in his bodily nature to the world of matter, in his life force to the plants, in the matter of sensation to the animals and in his higher members, to the Divine. Human and cosmic rhythm accord with one another. In short, man is the microcosm within the macrocosm. He is the answer to the riddle of the universe.

Man is a citizen of two worlds. His existence alternates between periods in a supersensible world and periods in the physical. He may live on earth for the allotted span of seventy years but before coming here and after leaving, he lives in other realms as a being of soul and spirit. His life is a rhythmic alternation of incarnation, i.e. living on earth in a physical body, and excarnation, living in a supersensible world in spirit form.

Before conception and birth, soul and spirit inhabit supersensible realms. At death they return. On descending to earth a soul-spiritual being unites, for its earthly existence, with three 'bodies' or vehicles, known as the astral, etheric and physical. In a sense these are substances, although only the physical is a substance in the material sense. The astral is the vehicle of sensation and the etheric the life force. (More will be said about these later.) The physical form is prepared by the parents and in due course it is abandoned.

An idea which is closer to many minds than that of pre-existence is that of immortality. It is enshrined in creeds and beliefs but what is usually understood by immortality is life after death. The individual human being does not relish the idea of his passing into a void and the thought of a continued existence is a consolation. At the same time it is an egoistic view. Nevertheless, if a person can visualise life after death, it should be possible to consider the corollary — life before birth. This is necessary if one is to have a picture of the whole man.

Soul and spirit descend into a physical body but they do not come naked from the spiritual world. They bring 'karma' with them in accordance with past experiences from previous lives on earth. Karma can be defined as the sum of a person's actions in one of his successive lives which influence his fate in the next. That is to say that the incarnating human being has gifts, desires, impulses, potentialities and he needs and wants to progress according to what he has brought with him. There will also be negative aspects in his make-up for which he now has to compensate. But there is another point. What the individual does or learns is of consequence not only for himself both here and hereafter, but for the whole world, even the universe.

Cosmos, earth and man belong together. It is obvious that man affects the earth in an external sense but there is a much deeper aspect. Earth evolution does not just 'happen'. It would not have taken place without the human being in whom a recreation of substances and forces takes place. When he dies these forces are incorporated in the earth. They maintain evolution. They give minerals the power to crystallise, plants the power to grow, lower animals the power to exist. But not only is earth evolution dependent on man. There is a cosmic dimension. His fate and that of higher beings are inextricably bound up with one another. So the life of every person is of consequence and this is affected by his education (or lack of it).

When we observe the growing child, we see, from week to week, from month to month, from year to year, how from within, forces surface which bring more expression to the physiognomy, forces which make the child's movements more ordered and orientated. We see how the vacant look in the eyes becomes more determined and how movements of

arms and fingers become more controlled. All these phenomena are a sign that a soul-spiritual being is taking possession
of the physical body and using it for its express purpose.

The descent into the physical is a gradual process. Observation of the early development of the human being in com-
parison with that of an animal teaches a significant fact. The
latter comes into the world almost as a finished product. The
gap between birth and maturity is relatively small. The human being is differently constituted. He has a middle period.
He needs time to grow because he is destined for something
more than transient existence. He can develop with inner
freedom his own individuality.

The Fourfold Being of Man

In contemplating the human being we are first aware of his
physical body but we know that this body grows and changes, accompanied by mental development. This physical
body is matter but it is permeated by supersensible forces.
Spiritual science recognises other 'bodies' or 'vehicles' as
enumerated above.

The physical body consists of mineral substances,
elements of nature, into which it decomposes at death. But a
living body does not decompose. It grows; it is sustained. A
force which is beyond the reach of ordinary sense perception
is here at work. It is something which man has in common
with the plant and it is called the Etheric.

In the human being there is also a vehicle of sensation —
pain, pleasure, impulses, aversions, passions, etc. This is the
Astral body although it is non-substantial. Man has it in
common with the animal kingdom.

The fourth and highest member of man's being is known as

the Ego. It is through the power of the ego that every man can say "I" of himself. It is through the existence of the ego that man is elevated above all the other kingdoms of nature.

Although every human being is endowed with an ego, it is not always active or developed in the same way. One has only to think of the difference between those who follow their instincts almost like animals and those who could be classed as idealists.

The human being is not at the end of his evolution. The ego can control and direct the impulses of the astral and the etheric and in so doing a certain transformation takes place in these bodies which results in the development of higher faculties. The strength of the ego itself increases. In short, the human being evolves new powers by his own efforts. An example of such a product from the past is conscience which is a result of previous work of the ego on the etheric.

In education these four members of the human being are of immediate concern. Although they are all present at all times, they do not develop uniformly and this is something which the teacher must understand.

Human life evolves in seven year cycles and this is particularly noticeable in the early years, for instance, at seven and fourteen. The changes which take place are due to the changing relationships among the four constituent 'bodies'.

Before physical birth, the human being is surrounded and protected by the physical body of the mother. At birth the body becomes free, enabling the environment to work upon it directly. The etheric, astral and ego are still intimately connected with the physical body. This is the case for the first seven years. At the age of seven, one could speak of a freeing of the etheric; at fourteen, the astral; at twenty-one, the ego.

On entering physical existence the child continues the experiences he had in the spiritual world prior to conception.

There he had lived within the beings of the higher hierarchies. There he was an imitator to a high degree because he was united with the beings around him. Then he is placed in the physical world. In it the habit of being one with his surroundings is continued. This habit then extends to being-one-with, imitating, the people who take care of him.

Thus everything around the small child is of consequence. All impressions from the outside world affect him. He is not conscious of himself but lives, so to speak, in the outer world. The child is given up to the external world in reverence, in prayerful devotion. It is a religious element. The adult arrests impressions from the outer world at the surface of his body — in the sense organs — but individual sense organs in the child are not yet awake. One could say that the small child is wholly sense-organ.

Within this first seven year period one can also differentiate three stages — minor reflections as it were, of the greater ones which occur at seven and fourteen.

In the first two or three years of existence the head is disproportionately large. Between three and five the main development takes place in the rhythmic system and from five to seven in the limbs.

Physical and mental development go hand in hand yet with apparent contradiction. During the first period, to about the age of two and a half, the formative forces concentrate on the head, shaping those organs connected most with the development and self-confidence of the individual in later life. The child learns to walk and to speak, developing powers from within but very much influenced by the surroundings. At this stage the expression 'wholly sense-organ' is most justified. The child's experience of the world is felt through its entire organism.

During this period three fundamental faculties develop —

walking, speaking, thinking. (The word 'thinking' used here does not imply the logical type of thinking of the adult but rather the faculty of creating mental images.) Divine powers are working through the child to bring it into balance with its environment.

Between the ages of three and five there is a marked development of the rhythmic system, i.e. the breathing and the circulation of the blood. Mentally the child develops memory and the power of imagination.

There is a change at the age of five. The milk teeth begin to drop out and are replaced by permanent ones. The limbs show more signs of growth. Slowly the child becomes more susceptible to recognising an authority. He looks up to adults, trusts them and can be guided by them.

The age of seven marks a more profound change. As we continually renew skin, nails, etc. so the child has, so to speak, driven out its inherited body and a new one has been formed after the pattern of the first, using products assimilated from matter and the substance of the earth. What has taken place is that the etheric forces have been active in organising the physical body. A certain stage of completion is reached as evidenced by the second dentition, and the etheric forces are freed. They operate now on another plane, namely in the formation of mental images which can then become permanent as memories. Astral and ego still slumber.

Within the second seven year period are also minor staging posts. At the age of nine or ten, the child becomes much more aware of the outer world and of himself as being something separate from it. At the age of twelve/thirteen, it is as if the spirit were penetrating into the bony system. Soon the grace of youthful movement disappears. The child directs his attention even more to the material world. At the same time the individuality begins to assert itself.

A major change takes place at puberty. Between seven and fourteen the astral forces are still closely connected with the physical body. All the child's feelings have a strong connection with the physical organs, with breathing, with digestion and with blood circulation. At puberty the astral forces become free. Sexual maturity is only one symptom of this. The other is the development of independent powers of judgement. The power of thinking develops.

At twenty-one the human being is considered to be grown up and self-responsible. Ego-consciousness reaches a particular stage.

Thus we can speak of a fourfold development, even of four 'births', giving rise to three seven year periods up to the age of twenty-one, ages nought to seven, seven to fourteen, fourteen to twenty-one. The implications of these periods for education will be considered later.

Body, Soul, Spirit

The four constituent parts of the human being already described are, so to speak, vehicles in which and through which other entities work, namely, soul and spirit.

We have already mentioned the fact that at birth a soul-spiritual being enters earthly incarnation. Let us now consider what is meant by soul and spirit in the human context.

The human being lives in a world of physical objects of which he himself is one, but through his mental processes he also lives in another world, a world of his own making. In this inner world dwell the faculties of thinking, feeling and willing.

The experiences in this inner world come from two sides. On the one hand they come via the physical and etheric bodies and create impressions in the astral. If there were no other factor man would not rise above the animal since the animal follows urges and impulses instinctively. The human being has, however, a higher faculty. He can follow his impulses or not. Moreover he can formulate laws about the things he recognises through sense impressions — laws which have an eternal quality — and recognise that these things exist in their own right. They exist both in his mind and in the objects. As the body perceives the physical, as sensations arise in the astral, so there must be something in the human being which comprehends such laws. This is the spirit whose laws are first of all grasped in the thought life. As the physical body belongs to the physical world so does the spirit belong to the spiritual world, the world of the eternal.

That part of the inner being of man which is formed by a combination of sense impressions and supersensible impressions of the spirit is what we call the soul. Thinking, feeling and willing are all organs of the soul.

The soul is the intermediary between body and spirit. It is formed out of astral substance. It receives experiences via the body through the senses and via the spirit through intuition. The spirit working in the individual soul is the ego.

The Bodily Basis of Soul Development

In the soul there are forces of thinking, feeling and willing. They have a physical basis in man in his threefold organism of head, rhythmic and limb/metabolic system.

The head, together with the nerves that radiate from it, is the physical basis of thinking. (Thinking is used here in its widest sense and means the ability to form mental pictures as well as to produce logic.) The head is, in a sense, isolated from the rest of the body. It is hard and round. It reminds us of the dome of heaven. In its construction and position it is protected from the shock of the rest of the body's activity. Man begins his embryonic life by developing the head organisation. The head is the most perfect part of the human being physically. From its lofty position it observes and surveys the world around. It is a picture of the stillness required in order to think, to form concepts, to recollect. The head is a pattern of the form of the whole human being from a previous incarnation. It belongs to the past just as thoughts belong to the past. Even if we think of the future the thoughts are dependent on the past.

By contrast, in the limb and metabolic system there is movement. Limbs and digestive system have much to do with the outer world. Movement is connected with will activity and the limb/metabolic system is the physical basis for the power of willing. One can easily appreciate this by considering how the power of the will is paralysed by fear, when the limbs freeze and the stomach heaves.

Like thinking, there are many manifestations of willing, from the instinctive to the conscious deed. Looking at the structure of the physical body one can see that the limbs are radials. They reach out into the world where they perform deeds, deeds which affect the future.

Between head and limbs is the chest which, in physical structure, is like a half-way house. Within it are the lungs and the heart. When a person is stirred by emotion, heart and breathing are affected and it is easy to see then that this part of the human organism is connected with feeling. The rhythmic system is unique in that it never stops work in the living person. Only with death does it cease to function or, alternatively, cessation of function means death. Whilst limbs and head tire through activity and must rest from time to time, the rhythmic system goes on and on and on.

It must not be thought that these categories of thinking, feeling and willing are absolutes. The human being is a whole and in each of these activities there are echoes of the other two just as in the body the three systems interact. For instance, everything to do with logic is considered to be a function of the head — concept, judgement, conclusion. But only the concept is formed in the head, affirmation or denial belongs to the feeling element and judgement to the will. What is characterised here refers to main functions.

When a child is born, the head is relatively large. The limbs appear relatively small and the rhythmic system un-developed. The process by which the three bodily systems become complete is a rhythmical one. By the end of the first seven years the head is more or less completed and from that time onwards for the next seven years it is mainly the rhyth-mic system which develops. Then comes puberty and the harmony of the previous seven years vanishes in the ungain-liness of youth. The limb system develops.

There is, of course, an interweaving even in the physical structure. Each part of the threefold organism has, so to speak, representatives of the other two within it. In the head, for instance, the forehead and the upper part is predominant-ly 'head', the nose and surrounding parts correspond to the rhythmic system and the moving jaws correspond to the legs.

The process of development in the seven year periods can be easily observed in miniature in the head. The upper part of the head changes little in the first seven years, but after that the middle part develops and, after the age of fourteen, the jaw. The forming of the body is not completed until the age of twenty-one. Thus we can say that the body grows physically from the head downwards. There are formative forces at work which affect particularly one part of the organism at one time, then another. At first they work on the head, then on the breathing and circulation of the blood; later, on the metabolism and limbs.

It might be thought that the faculties of soul would follow in the same direction. In fact, the reverse is the case.

Observe a small child. He may not be able to stand yet but he kicks his legs in the air and waves his arms. As soon as he can get up, he is all action. This means that the first power of soul to be born is the will, albeit exercised unconsciously. With the development of the rhythmic system the child lives in the world of feeling and only when the limbs have developed does the real power of thinking manifest. Soul development is therefore from below upwards. Limbs, rhythmic system, head — willing, feeling, thinking respectively.

The change from one period to another is gradual. Bodily development reaches a certain stage at the age of seven, soul life is predominant from seven to fourteen, and at fourteen individual spirit begins to manifest itself. We could also say that up to the age of seven the human being is a unity of body, soul and spirit; from seven to fourteen twofold, body and soul; from fourteen onwards threefold, body, soul and spirit.

Stages and Regions of Consciousness

In the interrelation of the spirit of man with the body arise conditions of consciousness. When the spirit is within, we speak of wakefulness; when it is outside, of sleeping. There is also the intermediate stage of dreaming.

Waking consciousness is continually interrupted by sleep. Without proper sleep man is incapable of fulfilling his daily tasks. The ego feeling is destroyed. Rhythm is essential.

Remembering and forgetting are processes similar to

waking and sleeping. Remembering is the awakening of a complex of mental imagery. Forgetting is to let it fall asleep. But as in sleep a certain maturing of experiences takes place, so also in forgetting. Being asleep is not a blank in our existence and forgetting does not necessarily mean a loss. The waking state returns, so does memory.

Even in the waking state these conditions of consciousness are present, namely, in the soul forces. Thinking is the most conscious activity of the human being. In the head he is awake. In the will, by contrast, he is asleep. (One has only to think of all the processes which take place in our limb and metabolic system of which we are not conscious — thankfully.) The third force, feeling, is one where man is semi-conscious; we could say dreaming.

All these matters have enormous significance for education. The teacher needs to grasp the ideas put forward, continually consider and assess them, as well as extend his knowledge generally. It must be understood that the constitution of the child is different from that of the adult both physically and spiritually and the teacher must recognise the implications for his teaching.

FIVE

The tasks of education

It is a sobering thought that children will be affected in some way by whatever is taught and by the way in which it is presented. A wrong education destroys vitality and leaves the mind a prey to destructive forces. A right education will produce human beings strong and sound in both body and mind.

In a previous chapter attention was called to the way in which educational requirements have changed in the course of history. What is right for one age is wrong in another. It is obvious that today we need an education which meets the needs of today (and those of the immediate future), but we must first recognise what these needs really are.

In the child we have before us a being who has only recently left the divine world. In due course, still at a tender age, he comes to school and it is the teacher's task to help to guide him into earthly existence. The teacher is therefore performing a priestly office. He is mediating between heaven and earth, i.e. seeking to harmonize a soul-spiritual being with a physical body. This being incarnates in stages, giving rise to the development of different forces. These must be cultivated appropriately both with regard to time and manner. The result will be a harmonious development of the personality which will feel at home in its bodily sheaths.

Bodily health is important, not only for its own sake but so that the body gives least resistance to the will of the spirit. Education is concerned with bodily health as well as with mental — a matter dealt with in a separate chapter. But just as a human physical body needs healthy physical nourishment for its well-being, so does the soul need healthy spiritual food which is given by way of stories, ideas, religion. The body needs exercise and so does the soul, but the limbs of the soul are thinking, feeling and willing. These faculties need to be cultivated by a right educational practice.

Contrary to current ideas it is not the task of education to guide a child into a profession. Given an education which embraces his whole being and enables him to find his right path in life, there is no need to choose a career. It will come naturally. In our present state of evolution, that is, in the midst of our materialistic civilisation, the essential thing for the individual is not to acquire more factual knowledge, even in the technical field, as some would advocate, *but to find himself*.

It is hardly necessary to point to the impending catastrophes which a breakdown of the social order is bringing about. Science has outstripped morality and for the human being it is now a matter of self-preservation — not in the material sense (although that looms importantly large) but in the spiritual. He is bombarded by negative forces and needs the right education to recognise them and to develop moral fibre to withstand them. He is continually being seduced and deflected from his rightful path. Above all he needs to recognise himself as a spiritual entity, related both to the divine and to the terrestrial. His present 'self' is a result of the past; his future depends on what he is now. He needs to realise his destiny and it is the duty of education to guide him in the task, not to persuade him to follow some arbitrary direction.

Referring to the idea of karma, elucidated earlier, we must realise that the incarnated individual brings with it possibilities and potentialities as a result of previous experiences. It enters earthly existence to modify and add to its own being through the new experiences it gains.

The child has no immediate memory of events before birth but has the results embedded in his physical and psychological constitution. Neither has the teacher this knowledge although he may be able to 'read' some of it from the child. It follows therefore that one aim of education must be to foster the development of the individual's inherent capacities and to allow full expansion of the predispositions of destiny. The child has to be 'awakened' and the teacher is the awakener. This gives a different dimension to education. Instruction or teaching becomes not so much a matter of imparting knowledge or teaching subjects as using teaching material to develop capacities, release and enhance creativity.

All things are related to the human being and all things are of concern to him. He can only be awakened to all his capacities if he is given knowledge and experience of all things. Practically, this means having a comprehensive curriculum and introducing the right subject at the right time in the right way.

Sometimes the question is raised as to the possibility of pre-natal education. This cannot be addressed to the child itself. Certainly the coming child is susceptible to influence, particularly on the part of the mother but pre-natal education, if one can speak of such, lies pre-eminently in the attitude of the mother. It consists of her realising herself to be the instrument of the divine will and harbouring such thoughts and doing such things as are morally justifiable.

Coming into the physical world obviously necessitates

adapting to it and the child must therefore learn the necessary skills to cope with earthly life. It is essential in modern society to be able to read, to express one's self verbally and in writing, calculate and do a thousand and one things which demand mental and manual dexterity. These things must be taught but it must be repeated that the manner in which they are taught and the ages at which they are brought to the child are of the greatest consequence. The child develops the appropriate relation to life at the appropriate age. For instance, it is unnatural to require a child in its sixth or seventh year to copy the signs which we now use in reading and writing, a matter which will be further explained in a later chapter.

Education must enable children to cope with life and stand on their own two feet. Hence, throughout school life they must learn not only the subjects which require mental activity but they ought also to practise the arts and learn all sorts of hand and craft work. They should be encouraged to make products which are both useful and artistic. At the age of sixteen something more is required. The young men and women need to be introduced to practical life outside school and acquire direct knowledge and experience of such things as spinning and weaving, industrial chemistry, machinery, mining, etc., the latest discoveries and inventions. They might ponder the question whether, or how, industrial products can be made which are also both useful and artistic.

The individual needs to find himself, to find his way into life, to acquire knowledge and skills to equip himself, but the individual lives amongst other individuals. Education is therefore not only a personal matter but one which concerns the community.

One cannot be a social human being without understanding other people's work, technical processes, or without knowing the great productions of human genius in the arts, literature, sciences and man's development on earth generally. The child must be brought to feel himself at home on the earth and belonging to it and at the same time appreciate the existence and the rights of others.

The social problems of the present time will never be solved in an external way. A solution will only come about through socially minded people and this means those whose upbringing and education have led them beyond the bounds of egoism. Social and political conditions are not the products of the state but of men and women. True spiritual life, of which education is a part, cannot be subject to the state, nor can it be dictated to by the economic life. It must be allowed to develop on its own in freedom. Only in freedom can education fulfil its task.

The aims and ideals here mentioned cannot be enforced. It is useless to tell a child he must be moral. A more subtle approach is necessary and the goals are to be achieved through educational practice which is detailed later.

SIX

Teaching in accordance with chronological development

We have already said that education must be founded on a knowledge of man in the widest sense — as a being with a physical body, a soul and a spirit. With his physical body he is related to the physical world, with the soul he has an inner life of his own, and with his spirit he partakes of eternity. Those who are responsible for education must also bear in mind the wholeness of life, the fact that the experiences of childhood have their effect in later life, not only in outlook and mental development but also in physical health. The whole course of life must be considered. What is given in childhood enters the forces of growth and continues to be effective. Hence great care must be taken of the how, what, when and why the various subjects are presented. The subjects taught and the manner of their teaching must be in accord with the development of the human being.

In a previous chapter, three stages of growth were described between birth and the age of twenty-one and although there is no sudden change, they can be clearly distinguished — up to the age of seven, from seven to fourteen, from fourteen to twenty-one. The figures given are approximate since there are always variations. Seven and fourteen are quite distinct staging posts marked by the change of teeth and puberty respectively (although these events now seem to be taking place earlier — Ed.). During these periods are minor changes.

In the anthroposophical view of life, a soul-spiritual entity incarnates into a physical body. The soul and spiritual forces which build up the body are present before birth and continue to manifest themselves in the process of growth. The teacher has to learn how these different forces reveal themselves and his 'reading' of the child will give the clue as to what is required educationally. This includes the manner and the order in which subjects are presented, bearing in mind that the child of one generation is very different from that of another and the fact that classes vary. We should not try to graft on to the child something arbitrary. Subjects and lessons should be introduced out of the necessity of child nature.

The first seven years, and particularly the first three, are the most important in the whole development of the human being, but not enough attention is paid to them. The school is obviously less concerned with the first period but educational indications are given here for the sake of completeness.

In the first seven-year period the child cannot be taught in the accepted sense. He should be more-or-less left to himself, particularly in the very early years.

Proper walking and speaking and the way in which these can be encouraged will be discussed in the next chapter on health but here it is fitting to give a warning about 'baby-talk'. The child will prattle and gurgle and make all sorts of sounds which are the beginning of speech. The baby's goal is to grow up and speak properly. It is not helped by adults imitating baby ways. Natural speaking, such as is worthy of imitation, should be the norm.

We said that the small child is wholly sense-organ. All impressions affect him whether apparent or not. The child will hear adults speaking and whether they speak properly and correctly or otherwise will affect him, but important is also that which may not be spoken. Expressions of fury or anger in the child's presence are obviously to be avoided, but so is the attitude which gives rise to them. It must be remembered that these things can not only cause immediate breathing or digestive troubles but that the effects linger for the whole of life.

Furthermore, if the child is in contact with people who have difficulties and problems, he will not only sense the atmosphere but imitate the physical effects; for example, in the case of contact with a depressed person, the child will pull a long face. Teachers and parents should be aware of these things.

Those who have ever tried to argue with a small child will know how hopeless it is. It is equally useless to preach morals. Words and admonitions make no impression, least of all pious formulae. The child lives in the will element and will readily follow an example. The key words therefore for the education of the young child are example and imitation.

If we observe children at play, we see that they are engaged in very serious business and if observation were continued long enough it would be seen that the way in which a child plays before the age of seven is reflected in the way that same person tackles life in the twenties. An intense and devoted activity in the child is reflected in a similar application to duties and tasks later. Similarly, the child's urge to explore becomes the adult's capacity to take initiative. Devotion to an ideal can only arise in grown-ups if they experienced total absorption as children.

Work for the adult is usually determined from without; the child's play is determined from within, from the being which wants to unfold. The child at play wants to imitate what is going on around him and he should be left, within reason, to his own initiative. Organised games are not play in the true sense.

In play the will is active and will-activity is characteristic of the early years. No boy ever expresses the wish to be a philologist but would willingly become an engine-driver. Why is this? The reason is that the latter is concerned with an activity which appeals to the senses and stirs the will. Anything intellectual is too far away.

For those who have a real understanding of child nature it is painful to see the sort of toys that are given to children these days. Even those which are seemingly innocuous, such as the usual boxes of bricks, have draw-backs and are not to be recommended. The objection is that regular shapes limit and define the imagination. Many so-called toys are inartistic to the point of being repulsive, in shape, in form, and in concept. Some have mechanisms, but the child does not want a mechanical contraption; he wants something to pull or push.

Among other fatuities are the so-called 'beautiful' dolls. They do harm to the child's soul because they leave nothing to the imagination, which is therefore stultified. A simple rag doll, even a handkerchief with two dots for eyes, is preferable and gives greater pleasure. It calls forth imaginative powers from the child to complete the picture and this is an inner formative power which also builds up the organs of the body. Education will foster perceptive thinking in adult life only if it stimulates fantasy in childhood.

When we plough, make hats or clothes, we incorporate an idea which has a purpose and also an outward appearance. This is a thought to bear in mind when we construct playthings for children.

Sometimes the question of memory training is raised. It would be demanding too much of the child at this stage to introduce memory exercises. The best thing for these early years is to stimulate the imaginative faculty by the provision of suitable toys and by the telling of suitable stories such as the fairy tales of the brothers Grimm.

If one is to speak of education at this tender age, then it is those surrounding the child who need to educate themselves, remembering that the child imitates what takes place around it, remembering also that the child is susceptible to 'atmosphere'. It is the duty of parents or those caring for the children to be worthy of imitation and to provide the right physical and moral environment. They should not instruct but pay attention to what they do themselves.

The child is not ready for school proper until the change of teeth but could enjoy a year or two in a kindergarten prior to this where suitable activities should be organised. Imitation of what the grown-up does prepares the child for later life. Children should imitate sensible activities. Objects in the kindergarten ought to be taken from actual life, not be invented by an intellectual manner of thinking. Cutting out bits of paper, arranging sticks, etc. hinder the child from growing into actual life. What is 'contrived' is no good for the child. He is best left in a gentle dream-like existence for as long as possible.

In a previous chapter reference was made to the great change which takes place at the age of seven. The coming of the second teeth is symptomatic of a development of the whole organism. The first teeth are inherited but the second are the person's own, adapted for use in the world. A stage of completion is reached and the formative forces concentrate their activity elsewhere. From the sleeping and dreaming life of early childhood there is now a certain awakening. Forces which were at the basis of growth of the physical body are set free and re-appear transformed into faculties of spirit and soul. It is with these that the educator must work, even to promote the physical.

In early years the child was an imitator. Now he becomes a follower. As yet he has no use for logic or demonstrations by proof but he needs 'humanity'. He does not want 'clever' people but fresh, lovable, artistic human beings who will care for him. He wants to learn about things in a kindly, loving way. The child no longer absorbs what he observes but that which lives in what he observes. Now it is authority which counts, not imitation. The nature of the child is such that he has a longing for authority. He demands of the adults the ability to believe in them, to feel instinctively about his teacher or whoever is concerned: "Here is one who can tell me things about the world because he is connected with it. He is a mediator between myself and the whole universe. I, myself, am not yet of that world." The teacher is the natural guide. The child looks up with reverence. The teacher says a thing is good, true and beautiful, and the child accepts it. Even in the matter of taste the child needs guidance (authority) as, for example, in the choice and recitation of poetry. The faculty of judgement is not yet awake. Behaviour can be regulated in the same way. There is no need to order the child to act in such a way. The child's own healthy nature will follow a good direction. In this way the ground is prepared for the future spiritual freedom of the adult.

Between the change of teeth and puberty it is the rhythmic system which preponderates. This is, of course, the main period during which the child attends school and a good teacher will be aware of the importance of working with this middle region.

Experiments have been made to find out how soon a child tires after one activity or another but if instruction is so arranged to fit in with the child's development, there is no problem. Let us remember that the rhythmic system of man never stops from the moment of birth to the moment of death. It is in the brain and the limbs that a man tires and must have periods of rest.

We said that the rhythmic system is the bodily basis of feeling. The fact that the rhythmic system and feeling are connected is to be observed in the act of blushing or turning pale, or fear which causes fainting, or excitement which makes the heart pound.

As the child is living primarily in the element of feeling, an artistic approach to all teaching is imperative. Artistic approach does not necessarily mean the practice of the arts — although that also has an important part to play in education — but that pictorial presentations are given through painting, drawing and mental imagery.

Pictorial presentation means cultivating the imagination. If teaching is pictorial the child takes in as much as he can absorb, as with eating and feeling satisfied. Some children take in more, some less. Appetites vary. Intellectual explanations make the child dull. Concepts and definitions given too early stifle and limit the expansion of the soul. Imaginative teaching stimulates not only the mind but also the fluidic forces of the body, promoting health. An example of what is meant by giving the child mental pictures would be — let us say — if one wants to give the idea of immortality. The image that one can use is that of the butterfly leaving the pupa; thus it is with the soul at death. To encourage flexibility of the mind one might consider how the tadpole turns into a frog or how the leaf can be looked upon as the fundamental principle of the plant which is transformed into the other parts.

(Goethe's metamorphosis of the plant.)

This artistic imaginative approach has a beneficial effect on the other two soul forces which are as yet dormant. Stimulating the imagination is a preparation for thinking. At the same time it engages the interest of the child and this awakens the will and the capacity to remember.

Unimaginative object teaching leads to frustration and rowdiness will be the result. There must be training of feeling and will. Above all, if training is to mean something for life it must be continually expanded to connect with life and with the human being. For example, it is usual in the physics lessons to give all manner of demonstrations. In dealing with heat one could bring in the idea of overflowing heat in the human body, i.e. fever: in dealing with mechanics, the human structure.

Practice of the arts is, of course, an essential part of education. Art has a harmonising effect. Among other benefits the necessary repetition strengthens the will forces. When attention is paid to rhythm and beat in the early stages of musical education, a similar result is achieved. Giving the child some special work or task will further develop the will.

During the period seven to fourteen the memory can be cultivated, but not earlier. Development of the memory is not by concepts but by teaching in an artistic way as described. Concepts load the memory; artistic activity builds it up; will activity strengthens it.

One valuable ploy in teaching is to raise expectancy, awaken hope, desire, resolve. The child enters the world of feeling and this stimulates the will. The teacher might say, "Tomorrow we will talk about ..." Another approach is to drop some irrelevant remark in the middle of teaching a particular subject to retain a homely atmosphere.

The child also learns through veneration and therefore a

good personal contact with the teacher is vital. A child will accept a teacher's wisdom because he loves him but years may pass before he understands.

From the seventh to the fourteenth year the organism prepares for the awakening of love. Gratitude develops. Love awakens. It takes years while the child is still living in fairy tales and pictures and is still in a dreaming condition. Then love of nature springs up — for the plants, animals, forms and colours of minerals; then comes a greater consciousness. A certain affection should also be encouraged even in dealing with inanimate subjects, such as chemistry, physics, mathematics. This brings in a human element. What the child learns to love in the early years he will understand later.

In this period everything becomes 'language' to the child. Everything is full of meaning, even movements and facial expressions — hence the teacher's responsibility to act responsibly and with dignity.

Much can be given to children between the ages of seven and fourteen which they will only understand later. The whole of life must be taken into consideration. There is little point in trying to explain everything that one gives. Ideas need time to grow. A man who can recall from memory something which was told to him in childhood and which he now understands has a refreshing stream of power within him.

Between the ages of seven and fourteen are the minor staging posts of ten/eleven and twelve/thirteen.

The transition is, of course, gradual and individual but generally between the ages of seven and nine the experience of the inner world and the outer world is not so distinct. The dreamy stage is still discernible. The child may still blame the table for hitting him. He does not distinguish between what is inwardly human and what is external nature. They are merged. Inwardly the child feels an impression, outwardly he sees a phenomenon. He connects the two. The teacher must appreciate this and accept it. Because the child is still in this state, he experiences a living quality in objects and therefore the way to teach about nature is to let plants, trees, animals, hold converse with one another.

There is a very important point during the ninth year of the child of which the teacher must be especially aware. The child is becoming conscious of himself as an individuality and as something separate from the rest of the world. It is not a conscious experience but manifests in the form of doubtings and unrest. It is a period of uncertainty. The teacher has so far represented the world to the child. Now the latter has a subconscious feeling: "How does the teacher know all this?" He wants confirmation and it is up to the teacher to provide this. The teacher must give the impression that there is still a great deal of knowledge which he has not yet disclosed. He needs to enhance his authority and he needs something in store for this moment. It must come naturally and can be done by talking to the child and surprising him by explaining something about which the child had no idea until that moment. This gives the right atmosphere and is reassuring.

Physiologically, at the age of ten, the muscle system develops and parallel with it other distinct features. The child begins to feel even more his separateness from the world and for this reason he begins to have a sharper perceptive faculty for what is happening in the outer world. He will, for instance, notice a teacher's mannerisms. The teacher becomes a different person. The natural development should be encouraged and children can learn, for example, to differentiate between the different grains, make acquaintance with this thing that looks like a root, but isn't, the potato, etc. The child should also realise the wholeness of life, for example, the plant in its setting and man's connection with the animal world.

There come also to the child at this age the questions — "Who am I?" — "What is my place in the world?" The questions are not conscious but the child has a feeling of isolation and needs something to hold on to. This is where a human relationship with the teacher is so valuable. The child needs a model, a guiding authority, one that can also satisfy the longing of his soul. Therefore the teaching must be — as already indicated — imaginative, lively, full of pictorial imagery and given so as to develop feelings of wonder and reverence. Concepts and definitions at this stage will restrict the mind.

Towards the twelfth year the muscular system begins to serve the dynamics of the bone system. The child comes, so to speak, into his skeleton. This means a more definite relationship with the outer world.

At eleven and twelve the child can form intellectual concepts of cause and effect, hence this is the right time to introduce chemistry and physics; also to consider causal connections in history and geography.

Observing children of twelve onwards, one sees how they are trying to adapt themselves to the mechanical nature of the bone system. The formative forces have proceeded from the head to the rhythmic and muscular system and now affect the bones. In school, the child is now organically mature to learn about the physical sciences, mechanics, dynamics, and to appreciate causality.

Puberty is only the most external symptom of another complete transformation which has taken place between the ages of seven and fourteen. Whereas the growth of the head and the expression of will are characteristics of the first period of childhood; the development of the rhythmic system and feeling, the second; now, in the third phase, fourteen plus, we observe the growth of the limbs and the beginning of conceptual thinking. Whereas it is nonsense to expect a child to make independent judgements in the earlier years, now is the time when the faculty begins to develop and should be encouraged. It must also be realised that young people have questions within them which they cannot formulate. The teacher must be able to anticipate such questions and awaken interest anew every time.

Teenagers have little respect for authority. They think they know it all and want to revolutionise the world. They must be allowed to be boisterous if they are to grow properly. They feel that their urges meet with opposition. These cannot be suppressed but can be guided by what appeals to reason. The teacher must once more prove himself, prove himself to have knowledge of the world and mankind. 'Not known' destroys the soul of the adolescent.

The awakening to sex is but one side of a much greater development. It is symptomatic of a search for relationships with the world as a whole. The young person is now extending his interest to the whole world and to humanity and it is vital to meet this interest. The expanding consciousness of the adolescent must be satisfied with knowledge of the world in every subject, in its problems and in its riddles. In the absence of this, interest turns inward and becomes eroticism and lust for power (Machtkitzel). Now is the time to recall, to recapitulate what has been learnt formerly, and now to answer the question 'why'.

World surveys of history, geography, etc., will provide food for thought as well as such matters as the history of art, of music, architecture and religion.

A stage of awakening of all soul forces is characteristic of the adolescent. The ability to think logically and to form judgements grows. What arises in the sphere of feeling becomes idealism. The desire to act, to change the world, becomes conscious. The young person wishes to discover the world and find that it is harmonious and honest.

The adolescent needs to have plenty of substance in his soul (acquired in early years) which he can think about when the thinking forces develop after puberty. Otherwise he drifts and latches on to all sorts of nonsense. Teachers of adolescents must have answers to the fate of humanity, the significance of historical epochs, the meaning of present day events, etc., i.e., a philosophy of life.

Adolescence is also the period when the growing person has to learn to adapt himself to life. Hence adolescents need experience of the practical world: how products are made, how transported, how factories are organised, etc. Visits should be made to factories, coal mines, steel works and other enterprises.

When idealism is stirring along with the search for self, it is time to look at the social question: "What is my relationship to the community?" If the situation is not satisfactory then the realisation can be brought home that institutions are made by man. Man is not made by institutions. Human beings can be effective by devoting themselves to their own tasks, by preserving an open mind and by being concerned for others. The feeling for responsibility awakens and hence duty.

A point to be noted in dealing with a mixed class — and it is a matter of great social benefit to have boys and girls together — is the different male and female psyche. A boy of fourteen or fifteen does not know what to do with himself. Something feels foreign within him and he is puzzled, awkward and reticent. His inner world presents problems. Wanting to be a 'big shot' may be a concealing of the real self. Girls are more sure, confident and self-possessed. This can lead to cases of vanity and coquetry but the outer world is full of problems for the girls. The girl has an ideal before her. She has an image in her mind which is the standard for her judgement of value. The deeds of a hero will impress her. The boy is more concerned with the nature of things but is influenced by the personality of a hero.

Dealing with adolescents is difficult and even more so if their earlier education has been neglected.

All through school children should receive impressions of religion, morality and aesthetics. This is the best antidote to eroticism, which is to be oppressed by one's own body.

Youth ought not to be sent straight into work after school. It accords with man's nature to enter work gradually, preferably practising on models while still at school.

At the age of twenty-one the third seven year period comes to an end. Traditionally twenty-one is the age at which a person is considered grown up. The will becomes free. Before this it was conditioned by the organism.

SEVEN

Health

Spiritual science gives many insights into human development which are not usually regarded otherwise. It sees life as a whole and recognises that health (or its opposite) is intimately connected with education. It gives insight into the fact that the effects of education continue throughout life, not only in the mental sense but also in the physical. It explains connections between mental and physical activities and also the subtle effects of foodstuffs. For instance:

— The root of many of the so-called nervous diseases of the present time lies in giving orders to young children and then changing them.

— Forced intellectual activity in childhood results in a tendency to arterio-sclerosis in later life.

— Illnesses of a rheumatic nature at the age of forty may be the result of a wrong sort of play in the third and fourth year of childhood.

We said earlier that child play should be an imitation of sensible adult activity. It could be added that sensible activity is a healthy thing generally. When activity is purposeful, it develops the will.

Digestive troubles will develop in the adult if learning has not been grasped in the soul life during the vital years of seven to fourteen. Specifically, teaching grammar badly when children are only half interested will lead to intestinal disturbances fifteen or twenty years later.

Unimaginative talking also produces digestive problems and too much talking by the teacher can cause the children to have a migraine. The child should never be bored and he will not be bored if all teaching is connected with life. The teacher would do well in his discourses to make interesting interpolations.

When instruction is given to young children without an imaginative content, as, for instance in merely giving definitions, it has a deadening effect on the soul. Causal explanations given to children before the age of eleven are also harmful. Things may be learnt in childhood which are not fully understood but will come as a revelation later and then they have a rejuvenating effect.

Purely materialistic attitudes to life ruin the minds of children, making it difficult to take in moral and spiritual influences. Insomnia can result from an education based on the materialistic-scientific mode of thinking.

It is important to pay attention to a proper exercising of the memory in tender years. If it is overburdened, the result may show itself as gout or rheumatism later. If it is not exercised sufficiently, then inflammatory conditions of the organism may develop, particularly between the ages of sixteen and twenty-four. The symptoms of an overburdened memory are paleness and insufficient growth. Over-stimulating the memory causes children to grow tall and thin. Too much is being demanded. In the case of a flushed face, the memory is perhaps being exercised too little. Obviously close observation is required and careful judgement. Then it is a matter of finding the right balance.

The physical body portrays past karma and soul qualities are also due to pre-earthly experiences. A child who treads firmly on his heels denotes that he had interest in everything in his former incarnation. There is much to be drawn out of him. The opposite shows a certain superficiality. A great many things should be given which the child can copy.

Three activities are of prime importance in the early development of the child and they should be carefully observed. They are: walking, speaking, thinking.

The child should learn to walk before it learns to speak. If there is no equilibrium in the movement of the limbs, stammering is the result. Leg and arm movements form the foundation of speech. Observe how the outer rhythmical element arises from the movement of the legs; the inner thematic element is related to hands and arms. When a child walks steadily and sturdily it has the bodily foundation for a correct syllable division. Leg movements correspond to strong contours of speech. In learning to walk the child learns to form his sentences. If a child does not use his arms and hands properly, speech will suffer in inflection and plastic form. If there is no life in his fingers, he will not develop a true sense for the modulations of speech.

Walking does not only mean achieving an upright position. It means that the child attains to the equilibrium of his own organism in the world. The action of feet and legs is different from that of arms and hands. Through arms and hands the soul finds its equilibrium. Walking brings us into relationship with the earth below. It deals with rhythm and measure. Arms and hands bring a relationship to what is around us. If we observe the child walking we may deduce something of his character and if there is something negative, we can intervene in time.

Where there is a lack of normal functions, proper development can be encouraged but there must be no forcing.

A child can be encouraged to walk properly, to walk rhythmically, to move the hands and arms equally so, but that does not mean forcing the child. We can help but not compel. Forcing to walk results in metabolic disturbances in later life, between about the ages of fifty and sixty. The ability to stand upright, to move arms and legs is something inherent in the organism. It follows that nature will take care of such matters. At the right time the child will stand up, walk and speak. Interference with the natural process is harmful.

Good speaking, rhythmic speaking, has a beneficial effect on the breathing system and hence on general health. Speaking in full, clear tones is to be encouraged. A sentence should be spoken completely, giving each syllable its full due. Indirectly, the right formation of the organs of the chest is dependent on correct speaking. Correct breathing is the result of well developed speaking. Listening to music also affects the breathing.

Speech furnishes the foundation for the faculty of thinking. The child learns to think through learning to talk. At first the child repeats sounds, then words, then coherent sentences. The order of development is walking, speaking, thinking.

Loving treatment while the child is learning to walk; truthfulness while he is learning to speak, clarity and precision of thought as he begins to think — these qualities become part of the bodily constitution.

A further matter for consideration is the alternation of sleeping and waking. Little thought is usually given to sleep although man devotes one-third of his life to it. It is generally considered a blank in life but sleep is all important even if the human being is apparently inactive. Actually, the opposite is the case but he is active in another sphere.

Observing the activities of the human being it is clear that activity of the brain — thinking — causes tiredness. So does bodily activity but there is the one region of man which does not tire, namely, the rhythmic system and the importance of engaging the rhythmic system through teaching in an artistic imaginative way has already been described. Art influences the breathing and the blood circulation. The artistic approach gives the child a feeling of joy and well-being. The waking life is beneficially affected in this process, but so also is that of sleep. Cramming disturbs it.

Artistic activity stimulates a hunger for physical exercise and this is then best satisfied by what one might call 'natural' games — running, jumping, free movements in space. But playing an instrument involves a certain amount of physical activity and this is also healthy.

Sleep is very much affected by bodily activity but it is important what kind of bodily exercises are given. There are 'contrived' exercises which result in restless sleep and in the longer term are the cause of flabbiness in the muscular system. This is a delicate process which cannot be observed by ordinary physiology.

Although of more concern in the home than in the school, care should be taken that the child gets the proper amount of sleep. Sleeping too much will develop a tendency to hesitate between words and phrases. Sleeping too little means that words slip out anyhow and sentences disintegrate.

The matter of nourishment is also an important factor in education although the teacher can only be concerned indirectly via the parents. A balanced diet is obviously necessary but a few special points might be mentioned. If children get too fat, soul and spirit have difficulty in entering the body. If a child seems to understand then forgets quickly, he may be consuming too many potatoes. Potatoes deprive the middle brain of its forces and the thinking is adversely affected. The consumption of meat brings the child too quickly into its body. Coffee concentrates thoughts; tea disperses them. Alcohol provides a substitute ego feeling. As far as children are concerned, all should be avoided.

The tendency to certain pathological conditions can be affected by changes in diet but this is the sphere of the school doctor, who preferably should be part of the school and versed in the world conception here represented.

Another thing which affects children's health is the temperament of the teacher. This is dealt with in the chapter on teachers.

EIGHT

Temperaments

We have said many times that education must be based on a knowledge of man, that is, man generally. But the education of the individual must also include knowledge of that individual. In this respect one of the things to be taken into account is the temperament. It is often stated that every child should receive individual attention but for this to be most effective the nature of each particular child needs to be recognised. The temperament presents one aspect.

Temperaments are usually classified in four categories, choleric, sanguine, melancholic and phlegmatic, related respectively to the four elements fire, air, earth and water. Seldom, however, does one find a person of a single disposition. Usually there are two, with one predominating. The teacher should not jump to a hasty conclusion since there may be other factors which might mislead, such as health and home circumstances. He or she has to cultivate a sharp perception, observe over a period of time and take many things into consideration.

A person with a choleric temperament is usually one who knows everything better, is aggressive and wants to order everything and everybody. He is very sure of himself, with a great amount of initiative and energy. In some respects he retains something of babyhood, with petulant outbursts if things are not done his way and visible signs of impatience, to say nothing of intolerance.

The therapeutic treatment in school is to have his energy exhausted. He must be provided with the right sort of stories and the right amount of action. If the teacher is sufficiently perceptive, he will notice a certain restlessness developing in such a child and will deflect the energy into a suitable channel before it explodes. Above all the teacher must be able to see the funny side of things.

The sanguine child has a very active rhythmic system, too active possibly. He rushes from impression to impression without grasping anything fundamentally. This gives him a certain superficiality. He feels restricted if he has to concentrate on anything for long and would prefer, like the butterfly, to flutter hither and thither.

The way to deal with sanguine children is similar to that suggested for the cholerics (and others). As the choleric must be given sufficient activity to exhaust him, so the sanguine must be given a multitude of impressions with lots of things to interest him. Eventually the abundance will exhaust and steady him.

The melancholic is difficult to approach and patience is needed. A child of this nature is weighed down by his own bodily organism. He is usually quiet and withdrawn, mainly preoccupied by his own condition, moody, introspective, showing little interest in the world around. It is useless, indeed harmful, to try to cheer up such a child, draw him out by funny stories or jolly him along. More likely than not he will withdraw disdainfully into himself and remain entirely indifferent.

A child of this type also has to be approached in his own mood. For him life is serious and full of cares and sorrows.

Given ideas or stories concerned with such matters, the melancholic will develop sympathy and a certain fellow feeling. This acts as a sort of release and his burden is lifted in the knowledge of the experience of others.

It is the bodily formative forces which are most influential in the phlegmatic. He watches the world roll by without getting too excited about it. He is a steady, reliable, careful person, has great potentialities but needs to be aroused.

In dealing with children of this type, it is again a matter of treating like with like. The teacher has to put on a phlegmatic act and this will so bore the child that he wakes up.

In dealing with the class as a whole the same homoeopathic principle applies. Sit cholerics with cholerics and they will mutually wear one another down. Sanguines will tire of one another, so will melancholics. Phlegmatics will awaken phlegmatics. In all cases a certain balance is achieved. A further advantage of this arrangement is that the teacher has a good survey of the class and knows in which direction to cast the sharpest eye. He should address individual children or temperament groups in a way characteristic of their temperament.

Where possible, too, he can direct the content of his discourse or a suitable part of that content, to the different groups, e.g. in talking about plants, speaking about blossom should be directed to the sanguines; the leaf, to the melancholics; the root, to the cholerics. The phlegmatics will appreciate the whole. (See Mathematics.)

There are cases where the temperament is too one-sided and verges on the pathological. It is then necessary to consult the parents and the school doctor as general health and diet factors may have to be considered.

NINE

Moral education

(The present climate of crime and violence makes this chapter of special importance. If a sense of morality could be developed in children at an early age, then a great many modern social ills would disappear. Ed.)

Morality is not something which can be instilled from outside. It is true that sets of rules can be established and children can be forced to obey them; but morality is only possible if it comes from the inner being. A certain discipline can be established in the school but when a person has left he must feel free. In his freedom he must know the difference between right and wrong.

When children come to school, they will already have been exposed to parental influence and if this has not been good, then the task of the teacher is so much harder. Bearing in mind what has been said about the child as a sense-organ in the early years, it is to be hoped that he (or she) has been in the care of honest, truthful people. However, the teacher has to accept the children as they are.

Speech and speaking have an important part to play in moral education. The way a child speaks shows a great deal of its character and the way in which it is addressed is character forming. Thus it behoves the teacher to speak properly, to cultivate his own speaking and thus set a good example. The word and its sense give direction. It is not only a matter of *what* the teacher says but *how* he says it.

To inculcate morality in children three primary virtues must be developed. These are: gratitude, love, duty.

The beginning of moral education (as well as religious) lies in the cultivation of the feeling of gratitude. It should be implanted in the first period of life when the growth forces are active, when a bodily-religious atmosphere envelops the child and when the impulse to imitate is still active. The feeling of gratitude should be directed not only to the people and the world around but also to the divine beings who are the founding and sustaining powers of the universe. In the early years it can only be done by example. One cannot achieve much with small children by telling them to be grateful. Gratitude has to be demonstrated in the lives of those around them. It is a matter of saying "thank you" not only to fellow human beings but also to the higher powers — for instance, saying grace at meals.

During the middle period, ages seven to fourteen, certain abilities can be cultivated which, if neglected, will be lost forever. It is the age when children become particularly attached to their teachers who, hopefully, are guiding their pupils into the world through artistic presentation of the subject matter — grasped in the soul life. Because of this connection and this presentation, feelings of love and respect are evoked which extend to thankfulness and love for nature, for existence on earth, for other people, for all that is good in the world.

Up to the age of fourteen the child has no use for intellectual concepts of what is right or wrong nor for dogma. Commandments may be obeyed outwardly but inwardly rejected. What is required is that the child develops an understanding for what is right or wrong through feelings of sympathy or antipathy. No morality can be taught by means of precepts. The child needs an authority in whom he has trust to pronounce what is good, true and beautiful and to illustrate it by material which works on the feelings via the imagination. Sympathy or antipathy translate into a feeling-understanding for good or evil.

Practically, this means stories or descriptions. The fairy stories are obvious examples. These are suitable for children in the five to seven year age range. At the ages of seven, eight, nine, one could use stories of animals in symbolic moral relationships with one another. Other themes would be those concerning human life and conduct where sympathy and antipathy appeal to the child's life of feeling.

This should be the direction of all moral education — one could say of all education — between the ages of seven and fourteen. The teacher must appeal to the feelings. The child must learn to delight in goodness and abhor evil; to love the good, hate the wicked; develop sympathy with what is moral, antipathy with what is immoral.

The adolescent who has received such pictures in childhood through the authority of the teacher has something moral embedded in his soul. The feeling for morality is anchored in his very being. With his growing powers of independent judgement the point of the stories can be understood and appreciated. The voice of reason is heard. The adult will incline towards practising conscious morality.

With the developing feeling of self and the capacity for independent judgement at fourteen onwards comes the realisation that what has been given requires service in return. If gratitude and love have been encouraged, there subsequently develops the sense of duty.

These attributes, then — gratitude, love, duty — are the foundation for moral education.

TEN

Behaviour

Some teachers have a natural authority, some can acquire it; some have no business to be in the classroom. Whatever the case, the behaviour of a class has a great deal to do with the teacher.

Bad behaviour is usually a result of boredom which in itself may be due to a variety of causes. If children's needs are met, they will be interested and there will be few problems.

Reference has already been made to the necessity of right presentation. This is basic but we would add the following particular points and suggestions as of some consequence in the matter of keeping order.

The principle of life is in- and out-breathing. As fresh air is needed physically so freshness and liveliness are required for the soul. Fortunate are the children whose teacher has a sense of humour. It is a great enlivener. In humour there is expansion; in seriousness, contraction. Lessons should have both their lighter and their weightier moments.

The teacher must seek to arouse moods of soul — tension, curiosity, followed by relief, relaxation and satisfaction. Lessons must be imbued with strong personal interest. This brings life to teaching and gets the blood moving.

Without referring specifically to behaviour, lessons could

be given in the normally accepted customs, conduct and manners of polite society. In cases where harm can result from certain practices, as for instance, smoking, the teacher can introduce, at an appropriate time, information on tobacco growing, history of smoking, the nature and harmful effects of nicotine.

In spite of the positive steps and attitudes enumerated, it must be admitted that difficulties will arise on occasion. Not all children are always amenable and not all children are angelic in their behaviour and some reproof or punishment may become necessary. Nevertheless, most children have a sound instinct for what is acceptable and for natural authority when it is correctly applied.

If there is bad behaviour in a particular class, an attempt should be made to improve the general tone. Much depends on the way a teacher speaks and on his attitude. Children appreciate firmness, consistency and the fact that someone cares for them, even if they do not always demonstrate this. The teacher must never lose his nerve. If he allows children to ask questions after he has been talking to them or telling them stories, to which he gives proper answers, his authority is strengthened. Not too much notice should be taken of mere rascals. If there is one persistent offender in a class, he might be made to feel ashamed in front of his comrades. If the offence continues, it becomes a matter for deliberation and possible action by the whole College of Teachers.

In the matter of discipline, petty rules and dogma do not go to the heart of the matter. An imaginative, corrective story — at least in the early years — will be more effective than anything. The story should be symbolic, characterising the offence, and show how such and such an action leads to the ridiculous. Allow a few days to elapse so that the offender does not consciously realise that he is concerned. The moral should not be pointed.

A classical example of a curative story with a slightly different angle is as follows: A teacher noticed that notes were being passed around the class. He interrupted his lesson and gave a discourse on the postal system. The children realised why such an interpolation had been given and felt ashamed of themselves.

If punishment has to be considered, then what is prescribed must have some connection with the crime, that is, it must be in the nature of making good. If property has been damaged, reparation in some form is due. If one child has harmed another, the perpetrator must be brought to see the error of his ways and be encouraged to offer compensation. With threats of punishment or a bad report little is achieved. Such practice as writing out 'lines' is merely an invitation to cultivate bad hand-writing.

There is also no point in keeping children in after school to do work that they have been brought up to enjoy. By way of illustration there is a story of a new teacher, some of whose pupils were misbehaving, and he threatened them with an after-school session of arithmetic. Unfortunately for him, these children enjoyed their lessons, including arithmetic, and the whole class wanted to stay behind.

Generally speaking, the class teacher arrangement, whereby one teacher is closely connected with a particular class over a period of eight years, has advantages when it comes to dealing with behavioural problems. The class teacher knows the children very well, and they know him (or her). If the teacher studies the temperaments of the children, he will acquire a useful means of exercising control.

ELEVEN

Organisation and homework

In the course of history it has become the practice in civilised areas for all children to receive an education. At the same time it is usual for the government or some delegated authority to be the responsible body. There can be no objection to a school being paid for from public funds but there is a great objection to education being organised for any other purpose than for itself. A school must be independent in so far as the teachers must be able to bring to the child what is necessary at every particular age according to human development. Lessons should not be conducted according to set rules, neither should the teacher be bound by prescribed goals. He must have freedom to cope with the varying moods of the classroom.

Naturally a school has to be properly organised. It is relatively easy to work out an ideal school plan but to put such into practice may be a little more difficult. One has to reckon with human beings and the fact that conditions change in the course of time. Flexibility is essential.

A plan may lay down certain requirements. It may be, however, that these requirements cannot be met. Teachers have different capacities and it has to be decided how to make best use of each individual's gifts. For instance, some may be able to give of their best with younger children; some, older; some may have special skills.

Ideally, the central point of any school, both in educational and organisational matters, is a College of Teachers. This is a corporate body of equals which supplants what is usually a headmaster and a hierarchy. It is the duty of this body to meet regularly, not only to discuss children and pedagogical matters but also finance and business. The arrangement does not exclude seeking professional guidance where appropriate. Such a body can, of course, only function properly when teachers are united in purpose and outlook.

———————

Three marked stages of child development were outlined in a previous chapter. A corresponding threefoldness is called for in the school organisation — Kindergarten, Middle School and Upper School.

Kindergarten. Up to the age of six or seven, there should be no formal education. Children can be accommodated in a Kindergarten and this could be looked upon as an extension of the home.

Middle School. Between seven and fourteen the child needs an authority and it is to the welfare of the child if he can look to one person in this capacity, a guide, philosopher and friend. It is therefore necessary to have a 'class teacher' who will accompany the same group of children throughout the period from the change of teeth to puberty, i.e. for eight years. When a teacher has been allotted a class, then the conduct of it should be left to his initiative. The class teacher is essentially autonomous. Other members of the college are available as consultants. (This does not exclude rare cases where an inefficient teacher may have to be persuaded that his talents lie elsewhere.) Teachers should not be afraid of large classes. Teachers and taught grow together in the course of time. In large schools there may be parallel classes and it is interesting to note how different they can be, but equally good.

The class teacher takes responsibility for the 'main' subjects, such as English, mathematics, history, geography and the sciences. He, or other teachers, could take the other subjects, languages, gymnastics, crafts, etc., according to ability.

Upper School. When children reach the age of fifteen, they are beginning to feel their independence and the close association with one person is now no longer so essential. Instead of the *person*, the adolescents will appreciate the person's *knowledge*. Here is then the field for the expert. Now, instead of the class teacher over a long period, Upper School classes need main lesson periods taken by specialists, one after another. One teacher could become class 'guardian' for a year at a time in order to preserve a continuous human connection.

It has been stated many times that in education only educational principles based on the knowledge of man are the decisive factors. This means a structuring of the curriculum and the time-table accordingly. Subjects should be presented in accordance with age and the time-table arranged to suit human rhythms.

Each group of children, each class, contains children of roughly the same age, that is, born within a twelve month period, and the age groups belong together. The idea of dropping a child into a lower age group because he has not made the grade is educationally unsustainable since all teaching, subjects and method, should be according to chronological age. There may be difficulties because children have different talents but the teacher has to find a way of dealing with these. In any case the difficulties often give way in the course of time.

The chronological development demands a definite approach to certain subjects irrespective of whether they have been fully grasped. To put a child of twelve with a group of eleven year olds is to provide him with the wrong nourishment. The argument holds good in the opposite direction. To be considered also is the bond between pupils and class teacher.

If children are really incapable, instead of being merely slow, then there has to be a special class with a specialist teacher who will help the child with his particular difficulty and, if possible, return him to the regular class. (We are not speaking here of really mentally retarded children.) To have a school doctor on the teaching staff would be an asset.

The usual arrangement of one subject following another in a more-or-less haphazard sequence throughout the day is not conducive to serious study nor to proper development of the mind. One impression is given, to be immediately blotted out by another. It is far better to have a concentrated period on one subject over a longer span of time. For instance, 'main lesson' subjects might occupy approximately the first two hours of every school day over a period of weeks, say English for three or four weeks, then mathematics, etc., aiming each time to achieve a certain stage. The other subjects could be taken in shorter periods during the rest of the school day but paying attention to giving the day a balanced rhythm. In principle, intellectual subjects are best taken in the morning when both teacher and children are fresh; active, artistic ones in the afternoon. At the same time there must be breathing space. A typical day might look like this: Main lesson — break — music, foreign languages — break — arts, crafts.

The day might start (beginning of main lesson) with a verse, song or recitation or all three. The verse should have something of the nature of a prayer and the Lord's prayer is suitable in older classes. (Original verses by Dr Steiner are in general use. Ed.) Singing or reciting together is a social activity which unites the class and enlivens it.

It is the normal practice in schools to give reports. These may be made every term or at the end of the school year. Often a figure or a letter relating to each subject is given denoting the degree of attainment: A or 1 = Excellent; B or 2 = Very good; etc. Such indications have very little meaning.

A report may give parents some information but essentially it is for the child. It should be something like an account of the experiences which teachers have had with the children but should also look to the future. To some extent every child is known to every teacher so all teachers concerned would contribute something to the report. The greater part, however, is the concern of the class teacher and the class teacher, knowing best the strengths and weaknesses, successes and failures of each child, would do well to compose a little verse or saying which is meant as encouragement for the coming year. This would accompany the report. The child can learn the verse by heart and recite it regularly. It will have a harmonising effect. Of course, this presupposes an accurate and intimate knowledge of the individuality of the child.

A school, particularly an independent one, needs the support of the parents. It is preferable for school and home to share the same ideals or at least for the parents to be sympathetic to the strivings of the teachers. It is of great importance therefore that the teacher keeps parents informed of what is happening in the school. It is of equal importance that parents show an interest in the school. It is of great benefit to the children if parents question them about their work and show an interest in it.

Parents' evenings provide one form of contact but it is also incumbent on the teacher to visit the parents at home where he can get to know the home background and discuss the individual. Being concerned with the general welfare of the child and from his observations the teacher may want to discuss certain aspects of health or behaviour, for instance, in respect of sleeping patterns or diet. Knowledge of the home background is also a help when it comes to writing reports.

Considering that the teacher is looked upon as the authority between the years of seven and fourteen, it is important that the parents support him and are not at cross purposes. Hence mutual understanding and co-operation are essential.

It is not only in conversation, meetings and showing interest in the child's work that the parents can give support. They can see to it that their children come to school in the right frame of mind and ... punctually.

Homework

From an ideal point of view children would master the subjects so well in school that there would be no need for them to continue working at home. However, one has to reckon with varying circumstances and conditions.

If children enjoy their lessons as they should (and will do if taught properly) there will be no difficulty about homework. It will be done voluntarily. Homework ought not be set, however, unless the teacher is prepared to mark it and, whatever the circumstances, *if* homework is set, it must be done. There can be no question of allowing children to avoid it or to do it badly.

Where examinations are concerned, it may be necessary to make special arrangements.

TWELVE

Teachers

The quality of education is inextricably bound up with the quality of teachers, of men and women with the right attitude and of the right calibre. Their work affects not only the physical and mental health of the pupils in their charge but, by implication, the world at large. Education can only be filled with the necessary vitality if teachers fully realise the consequences of their actions and methods. What they possess in the way of academic learning is of less importance than their ability to understand and to deal with children. People with their heads full of theories do not make good teachers.

Teaching children is a most demanding and responsible task and a heavy burden falls on those who make appointments as well as those who accept them.

It is relatively easy to set up a schedule of rules, principles and schemes of work but it is not so easy to deal with reality. The reality of a class in a school is that there are a number of children and a grown-up in charge. It is a human relationship. The teacher is confronted with a variety of children, of different sexes, different appearances, all with their own particular idiosyncrasies and possibilities. Every child brings with him his own particular character, temperament, potentialities, difficulties, stage of evolution, and physical and mental constitution, thus presenting the teacher with a great opportunity for study.

To take an interest in every child is an obvious requirement of teaching but interest does not necessarily come naturally. The teacher has to be trained, or train himself, to observe. On occasion children have been considered slow because deafness or shortsightedness has not been noticed. Eventually such defects may be diagnosed and cured but on occasion a step beyond this may be necessary to observe the deeper play of hidden forces. The teacher does not necessarily become a seer but he can become aware of the manifestation of supersensible forces and he can learn from those who have greater faculties. It is here that his studies of man and spiritual science will stand him in good stead. It is essential that he understands the being of man and knows what is demanded of him at every particular age. He will educate in the right way if he continually has before him a true picture of the human being and a realisation of the existence of a spiritual world.

The world and man are manifestations of divine spiritual powers. Contemplation of the natural world in all its wonder and beauty results in feelings of awe and reverence, but the peak of creation is the human being, so how much more do such feelings arise when we contemplate the child. It may require a conscious effort to view children in this light since they can become fractious, awkward, even obnoxious, but that does not change the basic fact.

A feeling of reverence towards pupils, even thankfulness that they have been given the opportunity of educating them is the right attitude for teachers in which to approach their tasks. It is a religious one and it requires devotion, love, enthusiasm, even when children are difficult. It is through this that the children, in turn, will develop similar feelings.

But each teacher also has this or that quality, individual capability and capacity, also failings. So for the teacher, education is not only a matter of being able to pass on the requisite knowledge, not only a matter of being able to develop the potentialities of the pupils, it is also a matter of self-discipline, self-development, self-education. At the same time he must have confidence in himself.

Many people at the present time are beset by doubts and uncertainties, but those who have achieved a certain view of life through their study of spiritual science are much more settled within themselves. They have a philosophy of life which gives them stability and sustenance. Furthermore, a world conception based on spiritual knowledge is inspiring. It combats the personal element. It keeps the mind fresh and is a source of strength when problems arise.

Such study as advocated also arouses the teacher's interest, his love and understanding. It generates enthusiasm which brings life into the classroom. It is a far cry from merely following instructions.

For self-development or self-education in this sense the teacher is recommended to turn to a book such as *Knowledge of the Higher Worlds. How is it achieved?* He will find indications for concentration exercises, for meditation and for furthering moral development; in other words, the ennoblement of the self. Such efforts at self-education and improvement will have an effect on the children. They will feel drawn instinctively towards their teacher. Uplifting his own soul will also help the teacher to deal with problems of behaviour.

The fact that teachers should exercise their minds as suggested above does not mean that they should distance themselves from mundane reality. On the contrary an other--worldly person, one living in cloud cuckoo land, is not fit to teach children. It is true that some teachers give this impression — not without justification — and it is strange that children are put into their care to learn, among other things, how to cope with this earthly world. Somewhere there is a lack of judgement.

It is an essential requirement of those undertaking to educate children that they extend their own knowledge and experience — that they take an interest in public affairs, that they participate in activities outside school. Naturally they must devote themselves to their own tasks and concerns but at the same time keep an open heart for the concerns of others. As representatives of the world in general they need extensive knowledge, an understanding of culture in all its aspects and of the general evolution of humanity.

Apart from such exercises and activities there are other factors concerning the individual teacher's character which need to be taken into consideration. How to deal with the various temperaments in children has already been discussed, but the teacher also has a temperament and that temperament can affect his pupils. For instance, a choleric person, with his sudden outbursts, may frighten children and cause them to feel anxious. That is an immediate result but long term damage is also a possibility. Disturbances in the circulatory and rhythmic systems may manifest themselves thirty or forty years later. A melancholic person is one living within himself with very little outflowing warmth. Under his influence the soul life of the child may be chilled and his breathing become irregular. Digestive disturbances and diseases of the blood may follow. In the case of a teacher with a phlegmatic temperament the likelihood is that the child will not be sufficiently stimulated. The phlegmatic displays a certain indifference to the world and the effect on children is a dulling of brain activity in later life, possibly nervous troubles and neurasthenia. The sanguine teacher lives in fleeting impressions. He does not help the child to concentrate, with the result that later there is a lack of zest and vital forces.

With an awareness of these matters, the conscientious teacher will try to harmonise his nature and to balance the temperamental tendencies. At all times he will be ready to acquire new knowledge and to modify his views in the light of what he learns. Thus he will avoid becoming dry and rigid. Absorbing new ideas and new knowledge is a pre-requisite for a fresh, active mind.

A sense of humour is a great asset. Unfortunately it is not a gift with which everyone is endowed and it is difficult to acquire. However, if the subject has been properly prepared, there may be moments when the material itself suggests a humorous approach and can be exploited. Above all, fanaticism has to be avoided. There are many views and opinions in the world, often correct but one-sided. Manifold points of view avoid fanaticism and acquiring these must be the goal. Teachers must be prepared to deny their own subjectivity and acknowledge the needs of the growing child as paramount.

After a year's experience in the classroom, a real teacher might realise that whatever the children may have learnt, he himself has learnt the most. He has the feeling himself of 'growing' along with the children, i.e. he is in a continual state of becoming. This is as it should be. However long he teaches, there is always this feeling, on looking back, that he could have done better. Anyone who does not have this feeling has been a poor educator. There is no finality in teaching and no finality in the development of the teacher. What is important is that he grows. His experiences with the children contribute to this but he also has to exert himself.

With regard to the actual subject matter — teachers must be masters of their material before they enter the classroom and for this they need the necessary time. There is so much to learn and so much to be taught that time must be spent in preparation in order to achieve economy in instruction.

Teaching is not only a question of pupils' interest and diligence but also of the teacher's interest, diligence and sincerity. No lesson should be given which has not been a matter of deep experience in the teacher, for he ought not merely to pass on what he has learnt in the same form. The material must be digested and transformed to suit the age of the child. If teachers repeat only memorised matter or teach merely out of a sense of duty, the child's development is stunted. A good teacher does not teach book in hand. Teaching from the book may well give children the impression that the teacher does not know his subject and they are probably right. It is not particularly encouraging for them to have to learn what the teacher does not know.

Once in the classroom the teacher has to give full attention to the children. His task is the artistic moulding of the lesson. It is to be hoped that he speaks clearly, properly, artistically — something he ought to have learnt during his training together with practice of the arts. Important also are the 'imponderables', e.g. the mood in which the teacher enters the classroom. Let him leave all personal feelings and troubles behind and let the lesson be based purely on its content and form. Let there be interplay between feelings of sorrow and joy, tragedy and humour. This allows the souls of the children to breathe.

We have already described the method of presentation of subjects, in particular the necessity for pictorial imagery and imaginative pictures between the ages of seven and fourteen. Beginners in the teaching profession may find this difficult but the ability comes with practice.

One thing must be emphasised and that is, as far as children up to the age of fourteen are concerned, the quality of the teacher as a human being is of overriding importance. What was said in the first paragraph of this chapter bears repeating: *What* a teacher is, is far more important than what he knows. Children need a warm, loving, human atmosphere. Sloppy sentimentality is not a substitute. Logic is, as yet, something for the future. Cleverness, particularly intellectual cleverness, is of no account. A happy, moral and conscientious person, with a sense of balance and humour, and one who naturally evokes respect and reverence, is the ideal.

In the state of adolescence pupils require something extra of their teachers. Young men and women coming into adulthood want answers to world questions as posed in a previous chapter. At puberty the young man or woman comes into possession of his or her own powers of judgement and the teacher must respect the growing independence. He has removed, or tried to remove, obstacles so that the person may enter in full freedom into life. It is to this freedom that we educate.

The teacher's work does not end when he leaves the classroom. It is obvious that lessons must be prepared and papers marked. He possibly takes part in extra-curricular activity but a greater and more subtle duty has to be fulfilled. It is a continuing duty of the teacher to have the children in his thoughts and consider how he can help each child to fulfil his destiny. He may put the question to himself: "Why am I called upon to help this child?" As a regular exercise he should let the whole group of children pass before him in meditation every morning and cultivate a perception of each child's mind and soul. It might sound like a lengthy process but ten or fifteen minutes are sufficient.

In the chapter on organisation, the advantages of one teacher being responsible for a class over a number of years was advocated. When this is done the teacher has a much closer connection with the children and it behoves him not only to think about them on a daily basis but also in the longer term. He reviews the children in his mind at the beginning of the school year and then again at the end. This is particularly important at the turning points of nine and twelve.

All teachers need the backing and support of their colleagues. Besides considering the welfare of children in his particular care the teacher has to think of the whole school. He can best do this if he has shared responsibility and is working with colleagues who have the same ideals. The idea of a College of Teachers was proposed in an earlier chapter. Regular meetings will provide opportunities to discuss organisation, pedagogy and individual children. Common study enhances unity. The members of the college should feel free to discuss their experiences openly with one another and consider suggestions without feeling them as interference. There need be no feeling of rivalry. Experience shows that when a difficult child has been the subject of discussion, the behaviour of that child improves.

A word needs to be said about teachers and society. Teachers are not always recognised by society as important. The child wants to look up to someone, to revere and therefore teachers ought not to be belittled.

THIRTEEN

English (mother tongue)

(Under this heading teaching material is included which is not, strictly speaking, instruction in English but which is used in conjunction with it and which also has a wider significance. The reference is to a sequence of stories which provides a form of spiritual nourishment. Ed.)

The first and the most important way of learning the mother tongue is through listening and speaking. Naturally children can already speak and understand more or less what is said to them when they come to school but the teacher has the task of cultivating these capacities further. Exercises in comprehension are something for a later period but practice in speaking is immediate. The child should be encouraged to articulate clearly, to pronounce all the syllables in a word and to speak in complete sentences.

Of course this postulates that the teacher has paid some attention to his own speech and that he has learned to formulate his own words and sentences lucidly, intelligibly and artistically.

Speech is something to be practised throughout the whole of school life but it is of especial importance in the early years bearing in mind also the health aspect.

One of the best ways of practising speech is by reciting poems, both chorally and individually. The best poems for this purpose are those chosen for their artistic merit so that the children develop a feeling for the beauty of language, a feeling that language is not merely a means of communication but a work of art. It is not necessary in the first place that the poem be fully understood and in no case should it be analysed until such time as the mechanics of poetry is studied in the upper school. Some introduction and preparation may be advisable before a new poem is learnt, particularly if it has the nature of a prayer. Children can very often recite a poem very well collectively, with everyone taking an active part, but they have problems if called upon to do it singly. The same difficulty arises in the matter of conversation.

At the age of six or seven it is not so easy for the child to express himself and he needs some stimulation, something which fires the imagination. Fairy tales are the ideal material for telling and retelling.

In the following year, ages seven to eight, animal stories and fables are to be recommended. Talking about the animals, describing their appearances and their characteristics is necessary as a preparation. Then the story can be told but in no case should any explanation be given or the moral pointed.

As the child progresses through school the ability to express himself, both in conversation and in writing, will undoubtedly grow. There is, however, still a central theme which is of special educational value to each age.

The Old Testament stories are the right material for children of nine; then scenes from Ancient History or Norse Stories (age ten), Mediaeval History or Greek Stories (eleven), stories from modern history, Rome (twelve), folklore of different races (thirteen), knowledge of peoples (fourteen).

Besides providing food for the soul, such material gives

ideas which can grow. The emphasis will, of course, change in the course of time, particularly as the stories become integrated with other subjects, but the following is important particularly in the first three or four years.

Let the stories be told in a quiet manner, without any dramatisation by the teacher, leaving the picture which his words have conjured up in the child's mind to be effective in its own right. Subsequently the children are encouraged to retell the story, or parts of it, but not immediately. Let them sleep on it. Before it is retold the teacher can talk about it generally but not seek to explain it or moralise about it. This talking should have the character of a free conversation between teacher and class.

Telling stories is much more effective than reading them. The 'teller' has to activate himself and this brings more life into them.

The skilful teacher will apportion different parts of the story to the different temperaments in his class; tranquil, quiet episodes to the phlegmatics; exciting bits to the sanguines, etc. In talking over the story he may also consider what he says and how he says it to appeal specially to each temperament in turn.

Naturally, using story material for telling and retelling does not exclude other conversation and children must be encouraged to say something about their own experiences. It may be that they have difficulty in expressing themselves or in remembering. Support is needed but not pressure. As the child speaks the teacher can interpolate corrections in diction and grammar. He will also be able to observe whether the child has been listening properly, bearing in mind that to listen properly is to learn to observe properly.

Writing and Reading

Correct speaking is a pre-requisite of correct writing. It will be noted in referring to these activities that the title is usually written the other way round: Reading and Writing. Here it is put this way because writing should precede reading. Physical activity should precede intellectual. When the child learns to write, particularly in the way advocated below, he is living more in the element of will, of movement, than in that of intellect, and this accords with his nature. Furthermore, writing engages the human being more fully than does reading.

The modern urge to get children to read and write early is harmful to their general development. If they have these accomplishments by the age of ten or eleven, that is soon enough. For social reasons or because it is customary they may have to learn earlier but it does not change the fact. Those whose education in these matters is deferred will probably prove to be the better writers and certainly more healthy.

Writing is a convention of civilised life but the letters themselves are mere abstract forms without, as yet, any significance to children. Let them therefore be taught in the least harmful way, i.e. artistically, giving the form of the letter some basis in reality.

In the first place children should be given the experience of form with the whole body. They can run straight lines, curves, rings, loops, etc. Then they can make arm movements corresponding to these forms. Next they draw these forms on paper. Colour can also be introduced so that the child experiences the line as a meeting of two colours. The teacher then explains how the sounds of speech are conveyed through writing. He takes a sentence, explains how a sentence contains words and words contain letters and letters correspond to spoken sounds. In sounds we can differentiate two varieties, consonants and vowels. He then takes a single letter, a consonant, and shows how it has developed from a picture, even if this is imaginative. (The writer recommends starting with capitals in cursive script. Ed.)

MOUTH   WAVES

The case is somewhat different with vowels. Whereas consonants are an expression of something in the outer world, vowels express an inner experience, a feeling. It is not so easy to demonstrate a connection between feeling and the written character (particularly in the case of the chaotic system of vowels in English. Ed.). Nevertheless an A (pronounced Ah) can be felt as an opening out, O (Oh) as an enfolding and U (Oo) as a closing in. One could derive the form from the shape of the outflowing breath.

It is not necessary to go through the whole alphabet in this way but to give sufficient for the children to realise that something real is at the basis of the letter. There is much scope here for the teacher to use his imagination; also, having taught a number of the capital letters, to lead to the small ones.

Learning to draw forms, a little more complicated than the

straight lines, curves, etc. will help in the artistic formation, as will also the completion of the other half of a symmetrical form:

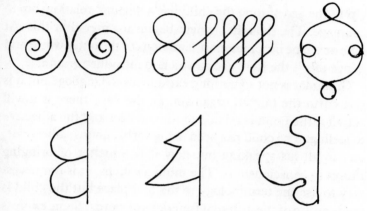

In drawing the forms of the letters children will derive pleasure from making artistic forms, following the line they are making with the eye. It will teach love for the surroundings and a feeling of responsibility. At the end of the first year they will be able to write down a few words or a simple sentence and at the end of the second, a little of what has been told or a short description.

Reading starts by reading their own writing. Gradually a transition is made to the printed word. (This is a recommendation by the writer. Ed.) The way this is taught depends on the genius of the teacher. When it comes to reading material, there is a difficulty in so far as most of the books on offer contain complete trivialities. A good teacher will bestir himself to find something more worthy.

Grammar

Up to the age of nine the child has a 'feeling' relationship to language. The thought element begins to enter after this. At nine or ten he becomes more conscious of the outer world and hence this is the right age at which to introduce grammar.

Grammar is not something extraneous to language but it is related to the human organism. In the verb there is a will activity; the noun is related to the intellect and the adjective to feeling. The child has been using verbs, nouns, adjectives, etc. in all his speaking but now it is a matter of bringing things to consciousness. The mind awakens. It is not necessary to use the terminology in the first place but the child is made aware of the different functions of words. Some express objects, some activity, some describe. Definitions are best avoided.

In the way a teacher speaks or reads a text, children can begin to learn syntax and punctuation. A relative clause will be spoken differently from a main clause and the voice will drop or pause for a full stop or a comma.

Teaching grammar and syntax are, of course, processes which continue throughout school life. Text books will provide the necessary detail but teachers must always strive to bring life into their presentations. Correct spelling is in itself of no great consequence but it is necessary for social reasons.

A few words must be said about reporting, composition and style.

Experiments show that few people can actually report correctly. Hence it is important to give practice to describing what is seen and heard, rather than to give free compositions. An appreciation of what is truth is of concern here. There are social consequences if the truth is not stated and children need to be educated to tell the truth. This is one way. Another important achievement is to be able to express oneself clearly in writing and therefore practice in composing business letters is to be recommended.

Children are not equal to writing free compositions before the age of puberty. Even then the teacher should first talk over the subject with them so that they write out of a certain mood. 'Aliveness' in the teacher must stimulate 'aliveness' in the pupil. Correcting is a matter of course.

Style is connected with aesthetic appreciation. The value of poetry has already been mentioned. At about the age of twelve children will become more aware of the aesthetics of language. It is again a matter of bringing certain things to consciousness. There are the different styles of poetry to be considered: epic, lyric, dramatic. Figures of speech lend artistry to the language. Sentences can be formed crudely or artistically. The sound element of language is something to be considered.

In the Upper School this study is intensified by having a particular period on Poetry as an Art which includes further study of sound as represented by the letters.

Literature

(Dr Steiner gave indications for literary studies but as they were for German schools, they are not entirely suited to English speaking establishments although there is much in common. A curriculum has been worked out by Eileen Hutchins, an experienced English teacher, which contains what is appropriate in Rudolf Steiner's indications plus suggested additions or substitutes. Details will interest teachers but for the general public the following outline might suffice. Ed.)

Some material for classes one to eight was already mentioned. To that we would add that biographies are very suitable throughout the school from the age of ten/eleven. They can be used in connection with other work. At age eleven, stories from Indian, Persian and Egyptian mythology are appropriate; then at twelve, stories from Rome, the Odyssey, Charles Kingsley's *Heroes* and all sorts of historical novels and travellers' tales in connection with history and geography lessons. These should include such stories as those of Charlemagne and his Paladins, Dietrich of Berne, Robin Hood, and King Arthur. At the ages of fourteen and fifteen, studies of Shakespeare and Dickens can be introduced; at sixteen, Greek Drama, Chaucer, Langland, French and German literature in connection with the development of man, also of literature and social history in the last three centuries. Some idea of modern literature should be given in the final class and a rounding off to complete a world picture as far as possible.

FOURTEEN

Mathematics

Whereas lessons on plants and animals belong to a definite age, arithmetic and geometry must be taught throughout the whole period of childhood, though naturally in a form suited to the changing characteristics of the different life periods. Algebra is not introduced until the age of puberty.

Although repetition and practice are essential and a certain amount of grind is impossible to avoid, no lesson should be allowed to become monotonous. It will not become so if properly formed, and the imaginative faculty is engaged.

A child can take in elements of arithmetic at an early age but the right presentation is important. It is even important for moral development. To start with addition, as is usually the case, leads to the idea of acquisition whereas subtraction and division, giving away and sharing, have an altruistic element and the child who first learns to share will be less egoistic. In any case life experience shows that man first sees the whole, then the parts; first the forest, then the single trees. This is the principle to be followed in the early lessons.

In Class 1 the teacher gives first the idea of unity and how unity can become plurality. For instance, a piece of wood, or an apple, can be cut in two or any number of pieces. Put the pieces back together and the whole is seen. A heap of beans is a unity, *one* heap. It can be divided into a number of heaps, either equal or unequal, or into singles. This demonstrates division and subtraction. Reversing the process shows multiplication and addition.

Starting with division, the four rules can be taken in quick succession and the processes practised with objects. The terminology is not important at the moment.

After the above introduction and demonstrable practice, the multiplication tables are learnt as a rhythm. The child is led to counting through rhythmic movement, using the fingers and imaginative pictures.

To give some feeling of reality to the ciphers, as with the letters of the alphabet, one takes the Roman numerals I, II, III, IIII, showing the number with fingers. Keeping the fingers together and stretching out the thumb gives V (five). An alternative to IIII is the more usual IV, that is, I before V, or V less I.

In Class 2 thinking and visual experience still go together. Questions and demonstrations are still connected with real objects. The time comes for simple mental arithmetic and the child's aptitude is best furthered by practising mental arithmetic before anything is written which, of course, demands a knowledge of the Arabic figures.

At the age of nine (Class 3) children become more aware of the world around them and arithmetic moves into the sphere of weights and measures. These provide the material for endless practical problems. Only after the age of nine can children begin to think of numbers in the abstract.

When the unity of the world disperses in the child's mind at the age of ten, that is the time to introduce the idea of the dispersal of a whole, i.e. fractions. With earthly maturity, i.e. puberty, the time is ripe for earthly matters, money transactions, etc.

Form drawing as a prelude to writing has already been mentioned. It is also a prelude to geometry. Through bodily movement a feeling is developed for form. Triangles, squares, circles, etc. can be experienced before they are drawn on paper. Reference was also made to symmetrical drawing (reflection) which stimulates inner perception. Also mentioned was the effect of such on sleep and health.

Before the age of twelve, geometry is mainly observation. What is presented pictorially in early years is understood intellectually later. Mobility in imagining forms, their transformations and metamorphoses, develops a feeling for space. Geometrical concepts are learnt from earlier drawing. The theorem of Pythagoras can be understood visually at the age of ten or eleven.

There is a change at about the age of ten from artistic form drawing to descriptive observation and practice using ruler and compass. Euclid is in order at the age of twelve.

The whole mathematics curriculum is something of this order, to accord with chronological development:

Classes 1/2/3: Arithmetic as stated.

Classes 4/5: Fractions and decimals.

Class 6: Interest, foreign exchange, percentage, discount.

Class 7: Square and cube roots, negative numbers. Algebra — introduction through formulae.

Class 8: Continue from 7. Measurement of solids.

Class 9: Combinations, permutations, linear equations, curves, loci, projective geometry, algebra.

Class 10: Progressions, logarithms, trigonometry, shadow constructions.

Class 11: Continue from 10. Mathematics and astronomy.

Class 12: Concluding survey. Practical applications.

Geometry in one form or another is a continual study.

FIFTEEN

History

For education to be fruitful all subjects must be presented in their relationship to man but history is usually taught as if it has very little to do with human beings. Facts concerning political and economic affairs are presented, wars described, kings and conquerors listed, dates given — to be committed to memory. Furthermore, the teaching of history is generally biased by a one-sided, nationalistic point of view which results in an entirely false picture being given. Another deficiency is that often only limited periods are studied and minds are thus constricted. The lack of a comprehensive survey means a gap in the understanding of the world and of man's development and consequent social short-sightedness.

A far wider view is necessary. History does not begin with some nationally important date (In England probably 55BC or 1066AD. Ed.) but extends far back into times when nothing was even recorded, but which can be understood through inherited mythology.

History is more than a succession of events. It is concerned with human beings. We are all part of history, a fact which is considerably reinforced if we can accept the idea of reincarnation. Events are symptoms of inner processes, of spiritually guided progress. In a comprehensive survey the whole process of the development of human culture should be shown. It is a false view of evolution to assume development from a primitive stage to that of present sophistication. There have been developed cultures from early times and real history teaching shows the sequence and achievements of the various civilisations , each of which has achieved something special. Past, present and future are interwoven and whoever sees a pattern in history can be inspired to work towards the future. The course of history shows a development from spiritual vision and group consciousness to a materialistic understanding of the world and a feeling of self as an independent unit. The question is, where does this lead?

While objectivity may have its merits in certain circumstances, a purely observational instruction in history creates superficiality, boredom and indifference to the world in later life. Learning facts by rote is destructive to the soul. The teacher therefore needs fire, enthusiasm and a capacity to mould his (or her) lessons artistically. Lessons containing lively descriptions and imbued with personal temperament will be inspiring but at the same time the teacher ought not to be swayed by confessional or national prejudices.

To introduce the child to history it is essential to awaken in him a sense of time. This can be done by appointing one child to represent the father of another, a third to be the grandfather, a fourth to be *his* father, etc... Holding hands one can form a chain and with thirty children in the chain one would be going back thirty generations to the time of Charlemagne. Then the teacher can relate some event or describe some personality of this period. Such teaching seeks to develop a personal relationship with historical characters. It appeals to the feeling and will of the children and to their imaginative faculty.

In general the method is to speak about the facts with

regard to space and time, then say something about the personalities concerned, characterising them and connecting them with what was already explained. In fact, biographies are a means of teaching history par excellence. The next day the matter is reviewed, considered and judged. This process affects the whole man, his thinking, feeling and willing.

Before the age of twelve the child will have little understanding for cause and effect, social impulses and the ideas which underlie them. Before this age, then, history teaching consists of giving single pictures of events or personalities. In the case of the latter, descriptions which awaken feelings of sympathy or antipathy through characterisation of good or evil respectively, are to be recommended. Children are not yet ripe for intellectual appraisal.

It is only after puberty that the child will begin to understand the great historical connections. It is in his nature, in his natural development, that at this age there arise questions in his inner being with regard to history. It is essential to cultivate a wide and comprehensive view and to correlate the subject with others such as geography and art. There is an added feature to history teaching in that an interesting presentation counteracts the development of eroticism. It is not important to give details of events but the great impulses should be expounded.

For example: in earlier years single stories may have been given in connection with the Crusades, or single characters described. After puberty the question which led to these great excursions can be approached and the results assessed.

Briefly: What led primarily to the Crusades was the secularization of the church. Godfrey of Bouillon wanted to establish a new Christian centre in Jerusalem as a counterweight to Rome. A vivid picture of the undertakings can be given — how there was great enthusiasm but no proper organisation

— how thousands perished — how the Crusaders themselves degenerated morally and quarrelled among themselves — how the Greeks became jealous.

In their objectives the Crusades may have been unsuccessful but they had a tremendous effect on Europe. The men who returned had seen new ways in agriculture and in industry. They adopted these and Europe became rich. New objects and new words relative to life style came into Europe — calico, muslin, sofa, mattress, magazine (in the sense of warehouse) tariff, i.e. taxes.

Moreover, the Crusaders learnt that there were Christians who did not acknowledge Rome; also that there were noble, learned, generous men among the Moslems. Apart from the introduction to material comforts, there was an immense broadening of the mind.

Other examples: The Graeco-Roman world illustrates the path to greater awareness of the physical world, to a feeling of individuality, to a new type of thinking. The legacy of this era works into the present — comprehensive, universal ideas and perceptions of art have come down to us from the Greeks; from Rome, jurisprudence.

The incursion of people from the East (The Huns and the subsequent migrations) brought about a tremendous upheaval in Europe. There was a great mixing of the peoples and where such a mixture takes place, new attitudes to life evolve. Then came the Vikings and one can sense the beginnings of a 'European'.

Of great importance is to cultivate an understanding of what took place in the 15th and 16th centuries, the beginning of our modern age. To be considered is the enormous change brought about by the Reformation and the way in which human horizons were extended by new geographical and astronomical knowledge; also the result on people's minds of the following scientific discoveries and the introduction of such things as printing machines. It was a period of expanding consciousness of the mind and ego development. Parallel with these is the awakening interest in art and literature, the Renaissance.

Obviously the advent of Christ and the impact of Christianity is another theme.

The outline of history teaching is then as follows: In classes 1 to 3 there is no history teaching as such: but among the many stories and descriptions of incidents which are given, some will have an historical aspect.

In Class 4 (age ten) there is a period called 'knowledge of home surroundings' in which the immediate neighbourhood is brought to consciousness in a geographical, historical, topographical survey, which also includes plant and animal life. Scenes from ancient history can be described and interest in individualities can be awakened.

Class 5 sees the beginning of history teaching but starting with ancient civilisations (India 7,000BC, Persia 5,000BC, Egypt/Chaldea up to Greek times by way of myths).

In Class 6 the history of Greece and Rome provides the right material, plus their legacy, up to the beginning of the 15th century.

Class 7 and Class 8 work covers the Reformation and the Renaissance, the periods of discovery and invention, also European relationships from the 15th to the 20th century. The period obviously includes the world-shaking events of the French Revolution and its aftermath and the changes brought about by the Industrial Revolution. In the case of the latter, emphasis is not to be laid on the trivialities of political life but on the way in which mechanical inventions and scientific discoveries change the world.

As children progress through the Upper School, they will

become more capable of understanding the inner historical motives.

In the 16th and 17th centuries came the transition from the older social pacts to the new political ones. In the 17th and 18th centuries the effects of rationalisation made themselves felt and in the 19th century there was a merging together of different peoples.

In Class 10 a survey of the ancient civilisations should be given, India, Persia, Egypt/Chaldea as far as Greece, in which period is the birth of philosophy, i.e. a new capacity, thinking. What was given in some cases as myths can now be interpreted to show the changing mind of man.

History sometimes overlaps with Geography and it is no great matter in which lesson some themes are handled. One such would deal with the dependence of peoples on the earth and their connection with the surroundings. For instance, people differ according to climate and zone. Mountain dwellers differ from those of the plains.

In Classes 11 and 12 the general survey should be continued and be brought into connection with literature. The centuries have different characteristics as mentioned. In the 19th century the spiritual heritage dwindles, traditions fade, but in the 20th there is a resurgence and new spiritual movements offer new insights.

SIXTEEN

Geography

The study of geography serves to develop a sense of space, interest in the world and social feelings. In geography flow together the study of the earth and the cosmos, of natural resources, economics and communications; of geological, biological and human living conditions; of spiritual-cultural factors. It shows the world as a whole. It has an expanding influence on the mind and it awakens other capacities in children. Above all it should arouse a feeling of brotherly connection with mankind in the various parts of the world.

In the first few years at school there is no teaching of geography as such but attention is drawn to all the different features of the neighbourhood (flora, fauna, relief, transport) by way of descriptions and stories.

At about the age of ten the period of study on 'home surroundings' will bring to still greater consciousness all aspects of the neighbourhood. These will include the natural characteristics, the way human beings have adapted or changed these for their own ends, the change that transport has brought about.

To lead over to geography proper the home surroundings study can be transformed into a map, a map with pictorial illustrations, using coloured pencils. That is to say, little trees are sketched, close together where there is a forest, and shaped differently according to whether they depict conifers or deciduous types. For orchards the drawings will be spaced out. Corn stalks can represent cereals, a cow in a field depicts pastureland while a car can be shown on the road and a train on the railway track. This type of map is to be recommended for all further age groups and in the course of time proper instruction in drawing will help children to produce good drawings of geographical features.

From the immediate neighbourhood the teaching expands to the nearer parts of the earth, dealing with the configuration of the land and economic conditions, gradually reaching round the whole earth and including all geographical concepts. The aim must be that children have an idea of the way the world looks and functions by the age of twelve or thirteen.

Between twelve and fourteen children are at the right age to learn about plants and their connection with the earth, how the face of the earth looks with regard to vegetation. They acquire a general idea of the structure, relief and climate of the whole earth, of its natural resources and how the gifts of the earth are used in agriculture and industry. A further important study is of the way people live in contrasting circumstances, together with their different characteristics, nature and outlook on the world. When studying Japan, a good exercise would be to encourage children to draw or paint in the Japanese style.

At the age of twelve an indication can be given of the three spheres of human activity. One is concerned with the processes of production and distribution, another concerns the human relationships with one another (rights and the law); a third with culture. In other terms, the three spheres are the economic, the political and the spiritual. This is an introduction to what can be an important theme in the Upper School.

Connections with other subjects as, for instance, with physics and chemistry, add to comprehensive understanding. History and geography naturally overlap and children can expand their knowledge by reading travellers' tales and descriptions.

Geology and mineralogy are closely connected with geography. Movements take place in the earth and the shapes of continents change.   By comparing the eastern coast of America and the western coast of Europe, taking into consideration flora and fauna, a connection can be established leading to the idea of the lost continent, Atlantis. Included in this study are ice caps, mountain folds, the formation of landscape in general.

From the age of twelve onward mathematical geography is a must, together with some knowledge of the heavens (zodiac, constellations, movement of stars, planets, etc.) — our present understanding of the solar system. However, before teaching the latter an explanation is necessary as to how one has arrived at this point of view.

The above is an outline of the geography teaching up to the age of fourteen. Adolescents should look again at the earth as a whole, the structure (the mountain cross — east/west range which includes the Alps and the north/south Rockies and Cordilleras), shapes of continents, creation and formation of mountains — everything of a physical nature. Further studies include isotherms, winds, ocean currents, the earth as a magnet, the earth's interior, the earth and the universe, map projections.

A final survey includes all aspects — geology, natural resources, economics, transport, animal and plant life, palaeontology, study of peoples, culture. Geography is the great mother.

Co-ordinate map-making with surveying.

SEVENTEEN

Natural History

(The term as used here is to be understood in a more comprehensive sense than is usual. It includes study of plants, animals, minerals and the human being. Ed.)

As a study, natural history can only begin after the age of nine when the child begins to develop a greater consciousness of the outer world and begins to realise himself as an individual and something separate. Before this he best learns about the world through stories and descriptions which appeal to feelings and imagination. To give all sorts of scientific facts too early has a destructive effect on the child's soul. Even at the age of nine or ten instruction should still be pictorially imaginative and only what is living should be dealt with, namely, the human being (in a very elementary way), animals and plants. The study of minerals belongs to a later age when, by nature, the child comes closer to the physical world.

Normal text books for children are basically watered down scientific erudition. There are others whose intention is to meet the child's stage of understanding but which are full of trivialities. Both have a deadening effect on the mind. The result is that the adult of later years cannot look back on such studies with any great joy, whereas school days in retrospect should appear paradisiacal and be a source of strength.

Subjects need to be dealt with in a living way. The teacher must also have a certain enthusiasm and not present his material in a dry, objective, matter-of-fact manner. Animals require to be dealt with in connection with the human being; plants in their relationship to the earth, the elements and the cosmos.

At the age of nine or ten the child has an instinctive sympathy with animals; much more so than with plants, which come second. Minerals need a different sort of understanding and they are best dealt with after the age of twelve.

The aim in animal study is to show that each animal species presents a one-sided development which is harmonised in the human being. As a preparation the teacher can speak about man's threefold structure and functioning — head, trunk and limbs. An example of one-sided development is the cuttlefish which can be characterised as all 'head'. The mouse is all trunk. From this point of view no animal is all limbs. Comparing the limb system of animals with that of the human being it is clear that in his limbs the human being is unique. He walks upright on two legs, leaving arms and hands free and therefore able to create. A man is only fully human when he makes use of his hands, when his hands are employed in work. As the cuttlefish can be considered principally head, so the lion has a preponderance of 'rhythmic' system; the cow is a walking stomach.

There is also the matter of soul qualities. In characterising human beings we say: as cunning as a fox; as gentle as a lamb, thus citing animal nature in our comparisons. In actual fact man has all these same characteristics but less one-sided, toned down, as it were. His nature is more harmonious and, of course, controllable. Without labouring the point it can be shown that both with regard to external form and soul qualities what is concentrated in man is spread out in the animal kingdom. However, man has higher faculties. The senses, sight, hearing, smell, may be more highly developed in individual animal species but man has the ability to reason. It is a great moment in a child's life, at about the age of twelve, when he realises this. He is then able to appreciate that the human being is a synthesis of the animal kingdom at a higher level and that it is within the capacity of the human being to overcome his animal nature. Hence, there is in this instruction a moral aspect which in turn, can strengthen the will forces.

In considering the plant world it is, again, not a matter of scientific study, but of artistic appreciation. Attention is called to the harmony and rhythm that live in nature. (In the early years the children will have heard stories wherein birds, plants, clouds, hold converse with one another as if able to speak to one another.) Growth is not merely a physical process. There is some unseen power within the plant which comes to manifestation in its physical form. It lives between heaven and earth. It sinks its roots downwards and strives with its stalk and flowers upwards. It is a living entity subject to the rhythms of earth and cosmos. It has a special relationship with the insect world. The root belongs to the earth and is of the nature of earth. The flower is ethereal and partakes of air and light. The green leaves in between form a balance.

In each plant the principle of metamorphosis is demonstrated. In flowers and seeds one often finds wonderful geometrical patterns. Nature expresses herself in a multitude of ways, yet it is one world that the plants manifest.

Whereas animal study should be conducted in relationship

to the human being, the plant must be considered in its connection with the earth in which it grows and with its surroundings. A stone is a totality and remains so anywhere, but the plant has not only the capacity of growing but its individual nature is conditioned by its environment. The forces of the earth are different in different parts of the world, so the beginning of plant study must be the geographical location. The growth of a plant will be different according to climate (wet, dry, hot, cool); according to altitude and, of course, according to the type of soil.

In learning how different plants develop in different circumstances the child's growing feeling for causality is satisfied. At the age of eleven or twelve, the stage of conceptual thinking is approaching but pictorial, imaginative presentation is still appropriate. In the plant world the child can 'observe' cause and effect. The process is a prelude to the type of thinking required to understand cause and effect in history. Hence plant study prepares the mind for an understanding of that subject.

The stages of plant development — fungus, lichens, algae, mosses, ferns, flowering plants — demonstrate a form of evolution. These stages can be compared with child development and be symbolic for moral development.

Observation is to be encouraged. For instance, children should learn the difference between wheat and rye, rye and barley; how a potato differs from a real root, etc.

Trees and the eventual use of their timber is a further study. To characterise the tree one could say that it is as if the tree had taken earth forces out of its environment and hardened them. Then, in a sense, a plant grows on the tree.

The vegetational regions were mentioned in the chapter on geography.

An elementary study of geology and mineralogy is appropriate at about the age of twelve, co-related with geography and plant study. Geology should be considered in relationship to plant life and the different features of the earth's crust be studied. In particular a study could be made of the Alpine regions where limestone and granite are neighbours. Mineralogy logically follows the study of rock formations, e.g. following consideration of granite one would proceed to look at the mineral content — mica, quartz, felspar. This follows the pedagogical rule of starting from the whole and proceeding to the parts, i.e. mountain, rock, mineral content.

A word of advice to those energetic teachers who take children out on excursions may not be out of place. Let the children enjoy the freedom of the out-of-doors without being 'taught'. Teaching is for the classroom.

After the animal and plant study periods comes a further study of the human being, particularly in connection with nutrition and health.

Reference was made earlier to the fact that between the ages of nine and eleven the child is essentially related to his rhythmic system and between eleven and thirteen to the bones, the skeleton. This latter period is then the right one in which to consider dynamics and mechanics because these things are now experienced in the body. (See under Physics.)

In the upper school the view widens. Appropriate now is an extended study of the human being and his relationships with the other kingdoms of nature. Further subjects would be: the mechanics of the bone and muscle systems, the inner structure of the eye, structure of cells, characteristics of races and peoples.

Anthropology is studied from the point of view of the whole man, not merely the physical. Botany is studied in connection with the soil and the whole cosmic influence.

As a final study there come the twelve animal types and again the relationship of the animal world to the human being. The pupil will realise that all realms of nature are a united whole and that man is the central theme.

Summary

Class 4: Age ten. The threefold human being. Animals and man. Animals are specialised in one particular direction.

Class 5: Animals continued. Plant study to show the plant between earth and cosmic forces.

Class 6: Plant study continued. Minerals in connection with geography and geology.

Class 7: Conditions of nutrition and health.

Class 8: Mechanics of bones and muscles. The functions of the organic systems and a picture of their harmonious working together.

Class 9: The nature of man, body, soul and spirit. Enlightened anthropology.

Class 10: From an understanding of individual man one can progress to the study of peoples — ethnography, also in an enlightened sense.

Class 11: The structure of cells. Botany as far as monocotyledons. The earth and the universe. The eye.

Class 12: Twelvefoldness in the animal world. Strata and fossils. Phanerogams. Man as a synthesis of the animal world and as a microcosm.

EIGHTEEN

Practical Life

Classes 10/11/12

Throughout the school there are many studies or activities
which could be termed 'practical', e.g. house-building, farming and gardening in Class 3; trade and transport in geography lessons: machines of one sort and another in physics;
surveying, first aid, bookbinding, gardening, carpentry,
writing business letters.

The social implications of understanding machinery and
the work of one's fellow men were already mentioned. At the
age of sixteen, young men and women are looking at things
with a different consciousness than in earlier years. Entry
into the adult world is looming and a gentle transition is
preferable to being thrown headlong into it. It is therefore
time to bring pupils into closer contact with the so-called
'practical' life. Naturally some pupils will tend towards the
academic side but it is good for them to experience the
practical. For those whose tendencies already lie in this
direction it is a preparation. Specialisation will come in due
course after a general grounding.

Hence there should be special studies of techniques —
agriculture, trade, industry, commerce, not overlooking

human aspects in connection with them. Special manufacturing processes could be studied, e.g. soap, paper, machine-made products.

A significant experience for the adolescents would be to use a real spinning wheel and a hand loom and then proceed to consider the processes in mill and factory. Working machinery of various sorts should be studied, including primitive types like the water wheel.

Shorthand, typewriting

(In the original curriculum these subjects were included for Class 9. Today they would be replaced by keyboarding and word-processing, possibly other media for communication, computers etc. Ed.)

NINETEEN

Science, Physics, Chemistry

The science teacher has a most difficult task. Natural science has become purely materialistic in its approach and the immense discoveries and their application in technology have produced a de-spiritualised and de-humanised world. To present a more complete picture much of the scientific knowledge of the present day would have to be digested and re-cast by the teacher in the light of his knowledge of spiritual science.

Natural science asserts that the earth and the universe came into existence as a result of the 'big bang'; that man has evolved from some lowly creature on the seashore; that a plant consists of such and such substances. To teach these things as facts is to give a materialistic interpretation of phenomena, which in themselves may have been correctly observed. It is one-sided and dogmatic.

There is an experiment whereby one drops a spot of oil into water, takes a stick and swirls the oil around. It then breaks up into little globules which swim around the centre. This is intended to illustrate the origin of the universe, but one thing of some importance is overlooked: someone has to do the stirring.

Spiritual science considers the earth, the universe and all

that is contained therein to be the result of the activity of spiritual beings. The book of nature is the script of the spirit. To present things in that bald manner would, however, also be dogmatic.

There is another approach as practised by the German scientist-philosopher-poet, Goethe. It is: observe, have confidence in the language of the senses, recognise in the phenomena the relevant idea. That idea is the spiritual entity.

The time to introduce physics and chemistry is at the age of twelve, the age of puberty, the time of physical maturity. At that age there is a change in the mentality of the child as well as in the physical body and the teacher gradually changes from giving descriptive instruction to explanatory. It is the time when children are able to understand cause and effect. The twin subjects of physics and chemistry are best dealt with as a unity, not an aggregate and, as with all others, they should be brought into relationship with the human being. Furthermore the teaching of physics and chemistry must always be connected with practical life. For instance: let the teacher strike a match. The children observe all the details, the inner and outer flame, the remaining black tip, smoke, smell, etc. Following the above procedure explanations would be given the next day.

The lead into mechanics would be by the use of the scales or a lever to remove some heavy object. If the teaching is not related to practical life, the children get bored. From practical applications one leads to concepts of weight and gravity.

Science, like all subjects, is not taught merely to impart knowledge. Concepts or ideas which merely enter the head have no life. The whole human being needs to participate. In earlier times one used to speak of the horror vacui, the horror of empty space. To be of educational value science teaching needs to arouse feelings, horror maybe, but also wonder and reverence.

A certain procedure will further the educational impact. The teacher demonstrates an experiment, then puts the apparatus aside and recapitulates the whole process from memory with the children's participation. The next day, when the children come to school they have in their heads pictures of what they have experienced. Now comes the time for consideration and reflection or judgement. The will is activated as the pictures become reality and the connections become conscious. This consolidates the affair and is a form of nourishment given before proceeding to the next demonstration. It accords with the needs of the child's mind at the age of twelve.

There is also a social element in the teaching of science. It is a tragedy that at present so many people use the inventions of man without knowing anything of the way they work or the effort required to produce them. It means that we have only a tentative relationship to our surroundings and fellow men. We live in a world which we use and have created but do not understand. We are stupefied by it and take little notice.

Better social relations will develop if this is rectified. Hence, when children are ready for it, they should be taught how machinery works, how chemical processes take place and how the rest of the world lives. Those are suitable studies for ages fifteen and sixteen.

Subjects recommended at the various ages

Class 6: Age twelve. Sound, light, heat, magnetism, electricity. Lead from music to acoustics; from colour to optics. Explain Goethe's theory of colour. Start each time with phenomena and lead to general laws.

Class 7: Age thirteen. Above continued with applications, i.e. dynamo, electric motor. Mechanics: lever, wheel and axle, pulleys, inclined plane, screw and applications to machinery. Observation and explanation of obvious chemical phenomena — rust, green on copper, decomposition of manure.

Class 8: Age fourteen. Hydraulics, aero-mechanics, climatology and meteorology. Chemical processes in industry. Organic substances and their importance in nourishment.

Class 9: Age fifteen. (Social aspects.) Steam engine, telephone, telescope, etc.* Elements of organic chemistry.

Class 10: Age sixteen. (See also Natural History.) Inventions, base, salt, acid. Study of limestone and its significance for the whole earth and in man.

Class 11: Age seventeen. Further inventions: radio, X-rays. (Television, atomic theory.) Substances in their natural state and then in living processes, e.g. sulphur.

Class 12: Light and its applications. Photography, magnification. Chemical processes in man and in outer nature. The universe as a unity.

---

* Rudolf Steiner died in 1925. The curriculum for Classes 9, 10, 11, 12, should be enlarged to include electronics, jet engines, space exploration and all modern inventions and discoveries.

TWENTY

Music

The frame of the human being is built according to musical laws. There is therefore the potential for making music and understanding music in every person.

Rhythm and melody are important elements in education. Even in apparently unmusical children there are musical tendencies which can be aroused. Every child appreciates inwardly the good feeling which music produces and which helps the breathing process. Music creates an inner joy. Singing is beneficial to the physical body. It is creative; it comes from the inner man, uniting him with the world.

At all times the aesthetic value of music should be cultivated and the child be encouraged to make music and enjoy it as an end in itself. All children will benefit from instruction although, naturally, it will be the gifted ones who become virtuosos. Private lessons or lessons in small groups playing this or that instrument will naturally be a necessity in the course of time.

The sequence of teaching the various aspects is related to the chronological development of the child as with all other subjects.

The young child learns through imitation. He has an inner experience of rhythm, beat and melody but a real grasp of what is musical comes at about the age of nine or ten when he develops an understanding for these things and also for harmony. Then music is experienced as something outside himself. The process is parallel to that of learning grammar.

Let singing be the starting point. The teacher sings and the children follow by imitating. A simple instrument, such as a recorder, can then be introduced and the children learn to play, also by imitation. At whatever stage is suitable the gifted child can progress to another instrument and have special tuition. An additional advantage in taking up an instrument is to further the development of the will.

In singing, simple pentatonic songs can be learnt before advance is made to more complicated ones. The aim of the first three years is to help the right formation of the vocal organs and to call upon the children to listen properly. Artificial, external methods of teaching are taboo. The child learns to listen, to imitate, and the teacher corrects. The organs are educated in learning to sing, not by any external means. To encourage listening, half the class can sing while the other half listens, then vice versa.

Music between the ages of nine and twelve is of particular importance. It is a regulatory factor in the breathing which in turn affects the circulation of the blood. It smooths out alternating periods of vigour and fatigue; sleeping and waking are harmonised in a beneficial way. It helps the will to unfold.

Before the age of nine, the child has no appreciation of major and minor but lives in the mood of the fifth. From then on an understanding of the third can be developed, then the other intervals up to the octave at age twelve. At ages ten, eleven, twelve, scales, notation, theory, etc. are the required studies.

At the age of twelve, coming into the age of conceptual

thinking, the child will be more conscious of music as an art and it is the right time to foster musical appreciation and to learn the characteristics of the different composers.

In the Upper School it is a matter of studying all aspects of music, including that of musical literature — past, present, and its creators — and cultivating musical taste.

In practice, besides singing and playing in class, various groupings are possible — a junior choir, junior choir-cum-orchestra, senior likewise.

TWENTY-ONE

Foreign languages

The gift for learning foreign languages deteriorates from the age of seven. It is therefore advantageous to begin learning them in the earliest classes, even in the kindergarten. As with all other subjects, teaching should be in accordance with the stages of growth. The choice of modern languages lies with the College and may vary from one school to another.

In the kindergarten this is, naturally, not an intellectual exercise, but the child learns the foreign language as it does the mother tongue, by example and imitation. The teacher sings, recites, tells little stories, makes gestures and acts, using the foreign words, and the children follow. Beginning at this early age there is the added advantage of easily acquiring a good pronunciation. Coming into the class teacher period it would be ideal if the same teacher can teach the mother tongue and whatever foreign languages are in the school curriculum.

One of the first objectives is to develop a feeling for the chosen language, and in the first two or three classes, ages seven to ten, this can best be cultivated by the teacher speaking. Whatever he or she teaches, however, must be from memory and not directly from the book. Best results are achieved if the children hear only the foreign tongue in the lessons. They can learn lots of poems by listening and repeating. They can recite them in chorus, merely following the sound element although they can be told the content of the poems. They can learn songs, listen to stories — ones which they already know are best — learn words and expressions for various actions, objects and experiences. Learning must be direct, not by translation. Speech and aural comprehension are more important than visual. Children should be encouraged to formulate their own thoughts in the foreign language and express them without the translation element, both in speaking and eventually in writing.

In learning the mother tongue grammar is introduced at about the age of nine and the foreign grammar can be taught in parallel.

At the age of eleven/twelve children may begin to read but the material should be something substantial and the trivialities often associated with language learning are best avoided. Some idea of the content could be given by the teacher in advance. Children learn best by reading, and if the material is humorous, so much the better. The fables of La Fontaine are very suitable.

From now onwards the children can be encouraged to write sentences or small compositions. A sort of translation might be practised in that the teacher says something short and asks the children to put it into the foreign language. Direct translation of long passages is to be avoided.

It is also part of learning foreign languages to know something of the people who speak them and the children will be interested in learning about their different life-styles and something of their literature. Proverbs and idiosyncratic expressions provide excellent and interesting food for thought. These studies, especially the literature, continue into the Upper School.

Latin and Greek

The so-called dead languages fall into a different category. Some knowledge of these is useful, even necessary for some pupils, and for those who wish to learn them the opportunity should be given. In general they can be taught from the age of eleven onwards as far as necessary having in mind the requirements of the particular pupil.

The approach is the same as with other foreign languages, i.e. through listening so that pupils develop a feeling for each particular language. Ideally, Greek comes first. However, since they are not languages in which we now converse, but learn in order to read the ancient authors, learning by translating is acceptable.

The works of the classical authors will provide the best reading material. A study of Etymology is advisable.

TWENTY-TWO

Handwork, gardening, first-aid

"No man can be a real philosopher who cannot darn his socks." (Rudolf Steiner.)

The purpose of handwork is not only to learn skills but to appreciate the many facets of life. Education needs to be comprehensive.

To cope with the vagaries of existence in this world one needs to develop many abilities. One of them is manual dexterity and along with that a knowledge of tools and how to use them. Any attempt made in acquiring manual skills is doubly rewarding. One not only acquires the requisite skill but the effort has a beneficial effect on the mind, e.g. when children learn to knit, it benefits them both physically and mentally.

Throughout the whole of their schooling children should be encouraged to make things, to be creative and productive. They can follow their own ideas, receiving guidance but not undue influence. Boys and girls learn the same crafts on the principle of appreciating how the other half lives. In the first school lesson the attention of the child is drawn to his hands and to the way in which human beings use their hands to work. All around are objects which are the result of the work of the hands of men. There is an element of social education here.

Knitting is suitable for Class 1, ages six and seven, followed in the next years by crocheting, sewing, embroidery. The aim is to produce simple articles which are practical, useful and artistic.

At age ten or eleven, progress could be made to knitting socks, gloves or jumpers, making stuffed animals and all kinds of dolls. At twelve, children can begin woodcarving and making simple wooden objects, also moveable toys.

With greater skill and experience children can, in the succeeding years, proceed to make garments for themselves and useful objects in various media whereby they will learn to appreciate work which is usually done for them by other people.

Bookbinding, metalwork, sculpting and carpentry are occupations for adolescents at the age of sixteen/seventeen.

———————

It is important for children (and human beings generally) to have a contact with the earth. Man is not wholly man without contact with nature and it is a sad fact of our civilisation that so many city-dwellers are cut off from her. It is incumbent on teachers to see that children get to know and to appreciate the great mater natura.

In the early years they will have heard nature stories of various kinds and will have been introduced to birds, animals and flowers. They will have had a period on home surroundings and on farming and gardening but the time comes when a direct experience of agriculture is essential — to learn the general principles of an agricultural system, maintenance of fertility, production of nourishing food, etc.

At the age of ten or eleven, children begin to take a greater interest in things of the outer world, they have skill and energy and this is the time to give them suitable garden tools and to instruct them in their use. They can then do some actual work if ground is available. However, if it is possible to have a school garden of adequate size, then the youngsters between the ages of thirteen and sixteen might have periods of real practical work for three years in succession in addition to instruction in the classroom.

An idea of first-aid ought to be given to adolescents at about the age of sixteen, one lesson a week for six months.

TWENTY-THREE

Art

Painting and drawing, modelling, aesthetics

Art has a harmonising effect on the soul and it has a great part to play in education. It is not only a matter of an artistic approach to the teaching of subjects, but of practising the arts themselves. For the most part they serve to support other subjects but they also require instruction in their own right.

In the matter of painting, the first thing is to arouse a feeling for colour. This is best achieved by allowing children to paint in flowing water colours, using a damp sheet of white paper which has been stretched and secured. For the moment the only instruction given is concerned with the technique — showing the way to hold the brush and use the paints. The latter should be ready mixed in pots, not taken from a palette. The teacher shows how to put one colour by the side of, or around another, using only the three primary colours. The children imitate this, then all consider the effect.

The child is then left free to paint out of his own inner soul experience without copying objects. Form is created by colour and the line arises where colours meet. The child will come to appreciate that there is perspective in colour — blue recedes, red approaches. In the first two or three classes the teacher can talk about the colours as if they were active beings. This approach to colour has the effect of stimulating the imagination.

By the age of eleven or twelve the child will be able to use colour as a means of expressing what he has learnt in other subjects. At thirteen or fourteen he will paint landscapes, sunrise, sunset, etc., entirely out of the mood of the colour.

The changing nature of the child at the age of fourteen/fifteen demands a change of media and this is met by black and white drawing, using charcoal. This takes the place of painting for a couple of years until a more conscious approach to painting can be cultivated at age seventeen/eighteen.

Wax crayons are useful for doing illustrations in connection with other subjects in the first two classes. Copying objects should be avoided and so should the drawing of outlines. Whatever is illustrated arises as a form from the application of colour surfaces. From the age of eight/nine onwards, coloured pencils can be used but this time the form arises as small lines are drawn diagonally from right to left, a shading technique. (Left-handers will draw the lines the other way.)

Besides using drawing for illustrations there are other aspects of the subject to be considered. In the early classes the drawing of lines, curves, loops, etc. is practised as a preliminary to writing. Form drawing (spirals, lemniscates, etc.) and symmetrical drawing awaken interest in forms themselves.

From the age of eleven onwards form-drawing gives place to geometry. At first the various geometrical figures can be drawn freehand, then with ruler and compasses. Simple projection and shadow drawing can be introduced. An understanding is awakened for the connection between the technical and the beautiful. Perspective is a subject to be introduced at the age of thirteen. At all times the cultivation of an aesthetic sense is important.

In the Upper School drawing is mostly connected with other subjects — projective geometry, drawing to scale, map making, surveying.

—————————

With regard to modelling, (plasticine, wax, clay) this is also used in support of other subjects. In itself it has a beneficial effect on children, particularly at about the age of ten. In shaping plastic forms and figures, modelling has a vitalising effect on the child's sight and his inner quality of soul.

There is so much in life that passes one by unless a greater awareness is cultivated. If a child learns to model, it gives him an experience of form through the hands and fingers, a tactile experience, not merely a visual one. It arouses a different sort of consciousness. In the course of time dexterity of hand has to be guided into the artistic.

—————————

In the upper classes the study of art itself is of great benefit.

Teaching up to the age of fourteen has been predominantly directed at the feeling element in the child. Now comes the beginning of intellectual thinking and comprehension in concepts.

When children are learning about the minerals, about the inorganic, lifeless aspects of nature, physics, chemistry, the laws of cause and effect, then a balance is essential and this is provided by a study of art. It should concern itself with the way the various arts have developed in the different epochs of history and how certain art-forms have manifested in certain periods. This gives further insight into the development of civilisation and humanity.

The following is recommended

Class 9: Pupils learn to grasp the concept of beauty or 'art for its own sake' and appreciate the change in the concept historically, i.e. What was the Greek ideal of beauty? What was that of the Renaissance? This is not done in the abstract but by taking examples of typical works. The study should be correlated with history and history of literature. The development of the plastic arts and painting is shown from ancient times to Rembrandt.

Class 10: The concept of beauty in speech. The word or sound is a medium of art. Pupils are encouraged to develop a feeling for this and for poetic forms.

Class 11: Music. The relationship of music and poetry. A theme for this class would be 'art in connection with the whole development of civilisation'. Questions to be answered would be, "Why did music, as we understand it, develop relatively late?" "What was the Greek understanding of music?" "Why does landscape painting begin at a certain time?" "What is the connection between art and religion?"

Class 12: Architecture. Starting with a consideration of the techniques of building, their development and materials used, the art instruction in this class is designed to awaken an understanding for the elements of architecture in its various forms and styles throughout the great cultural epochs of history.

In conclusion a survey of the whole development of art will demonstrate the underlying spiritual impulses.

TWENTY-FOUR

Gymnastics and eurythmy

Gymnastics is practised for the sake of good health but the manner of exercising has become very one-sided in that today it is a form of physical training devoid of soul content. It has developed from the purely physical, mechanical concept of the human being and whilst it is true that physical, mechanical laws are involved in all human movement, there are other things to be taken into consideration.

In practising gymnastics the child develops strength, agility and consciousness, but stereotyped exercises, imposed on children without their inner participation, are lifeless and harmful. On the other hand, exercises with content for the soul lead to a strengthening of the organism, even to healthier sleep. To educate the whole human being, mind and body must function together.

The physical body exists in space. As a child grows he has to accommodate himself to the world around him, to the world of space. To help him to orientate himself in this world is part of the task of gymnastics. He therefore needs exercises which develop a feeling for space and for direction, with something for the mind at the same time.

The human being lives in a balance between downward and upward acting forces. Gravity keeps the body on the earth but other forces hold the body upright. These are forces of consciousness. Children should learn, so to speak, to carry their body. To experience the line of the ego (one's own vertical axis) is a gymnastic experience with the soul content "I am." The gymnast experiences the 'static' and the 'dynamic.' Will power overcomes the inertia of the physical body. This feeling is enhanced in moving, particularly in jumping. The child's experience in gymnastics is "I feel growing power within me."

The human being also lives in a world of rhythms, reflected in his own body. Rhythmic exercises are also health giving. One has only to think of the breathing processes. Breathing-in gives a sense of refreshment; breathing-out inspires self confidence.

In the natural course of the day the necessity for physical exercise will be felt but the gymnastic lesson ought not to be looked upon as one of mere recuperation. It is a serious lesson in its own right but best taken somewhat separately from other lessons if possible. An afternoon period is probably the most suitable. A few minutes rest at the end of the lesson is recommended.

Boys and girls can well practise gymnastics together but perhaps, particularly in adolescence, doing different things.

In the first three years, ages six, seven, eight, there is no need for special gymnastic lessons. Eurythmy provides one form of bodily movement and otherwise children are quite happy to activate themselves, running, skipping, jumping or playing active ring games. A little organisation may be necessary.

From the age of nine and ten onwards children need activities which demand courage, determination and steadfastness. To running, etc. can be added rope-climbing, throwing, swinging hand over hand along a suspended rope.

They can have free play on the apparatus.

Exercises which imitate the gestures of human work are very suitable. These are performed rhythmically to the accompaniment of recitation or music. An emotional and imaginative relationship to the exercises is thus established.

From the age of fourteen onwards more controlled movement is required. More complicated exercises are necessary to develop orientation in space. There should be a conscious experience of what was formerly done instinctively. More use can be made of apparatus such as parallel and horizontal bars, vaulting horse, etc. Pupils experience joy in healthy movements of the whole body and in conscious control.

Eurythmy

(Eurythmy is an art of movement and to try to describe it in writing, without being able to demonstrate it, is a well-nigh impossible task. Ed.)

We can characterise this art by calling it visible speech or visible song. When a sound is spoken or a note is sung, there are certain movements in the larynx which are arrested and repressed whereby a sound issues forth. Imagine these movements being continued and manifested throughout the whole human being and we have eurythmy. It is a movement or gesture of the whole body which expresses the nature of the element of sound. Thus if a sound "Ah" is expressed, which in itself has the significance of astonishment, the gesture is one of opening out. "B" is the opposite — an enclosing. "L" calls for a gesture signifying an unfolding; "R" has a rolling movement. Every sound and tone has a corresponding movement and eurythmy is practised to the accompaniment of speech or music. There is no intellectual content. While interpreting the sound the persons concerned move in accordance with certain choreographic rules. Eurythmy provides, incidentally, a great means of training the sense of hearing. As in other arts the human being brings something of his inner being to expression, so in eurythmy, but his instrument is his own body.

As an art, eurythmy has an uplifting quality. In so far as it is practised in the company of others, it has a social element; in fact there are special exercises for cultivating sociability in children. Eurythmy also has a therapeutic and harmonising effect and furthers the appreciation of language and music.

TWENTY-FIVE

Religion

Religious instruction is not a matter of creed, dogma, or of peddling pious platitudes. It is concerned with an appreciation of the spirit which lives in all things. The human being, the world and all that it contains were created by God and are a manifestation of the divine. All subjects should be taught out of a consciousness of this spiritual background and in this sense every lesson is a religion lesson.

In former times men had direct contact with the divine. They had spiritual vision which gave them strength. They had knowledge but the direct contact was lost in the course of history and what had been knowledge became belief or eventually non-belief. What has been lost in religious experience is sought for today in sport.

Without religion no person is whole. Man is only complete when he is morally motivated through religion. To deprive children of religious instruction is to only half-educate them.

Religion and its associated attributes, morality, love, duty, are not things which can be instilled into children through precepts. They have to grow from within the soul. To foster them is one of the most important tasks of the present age. Religious instruction for children is useless if given in the form of knowledge only. It must invoke the feelings. The divine is not understood through wisdom but through love. Ideas must stimulate feeling and will. A religious mood is the goal.

If the teacher is to be a real educator he cannot approach the children with intellectual knowledge only. He must himself be inwardly religious, i.e. he must experience wonder at the growing child as a divine manifestation. He must have a love for the child and for what he has to do for the child. He must himself possess moral religious impulses and feel gratitude towards the divine creative powers. Anything less than this is a sham and the teaching will be ineffective. The teacher must believe in what he teaches. At the same time he has to respect the freedom of the child and not seek to indoctrinate him. He has to be careful to find the right balance. There are also certain imponderables. What lives in the teacher's soul has an effect on the children. Education depends on what the teacher *is*, not only on what he says. The teacher himself needs to be concerned for his own spiritual development. For those who would teach religion the above applies in the highest degree.

As in all subjects the material used and the approach must be based on the chronological age of the child.

Very young children have a natural religious feeling since they are still at one with their surroundings. As they grow they need the guidance and protection of adults. Before the age of fourteen they have no basis for moral judgement. They develop religious, moral, ethical feelings under the influence of others. They have no use for directives but will develop love for that which the teacher considers good, true and beautiful. Dogma and injunctions leave them cold.

A proper beginning for the religion lesson would be the recitation of a suitable verse, or singing, or both.

(Dr Steiner himself provided a suitable opening verse.

Ed.) Children recite or sing in chorus and there should be a suitable ending to the lesson — where appropriate, the Lord's Prayer. In support of his goal the teacher may find suitable poems or literary extracts, not overlooking such things as the Psalms, the Song of Solomon and verses from Anthroposophical literature.

For the small child all nature is living and flowers, sun, trees, rivers, etc. can hold converse with one another. All are animated by the spirit. The same spirit is at work also in the human being. The aim would be to inculcate the feeling that the divine, Father God, lives everywhere, not only in nature but also in man. That which is not seen becomes manifest. Elemental beings are at work in nature everywhere and stories of such can be given or reference made to them in conversation. It is the cultivation of the feeling which is essential, a feeling for the wisdom in nature, a feeling of gratitude to the world powers for what is given to mankind. Gratitude overcomes egoism and becomes love.

For the ages of seven, eight, nine, the aim is similar — to arouse the feeling that there is spirit in nature — but the approach changes. It is not yet time for philosophical discourses but appeal can be made to the imagination by the way of descriptions and stories. Fairy tales and legends will provide some material. Many fairy stories portray cosmic truths and human development, but in picture form.

Other possibilities are for the teacher to speak of events which are obviously life (spirit) processes. One example would be that of human development, from baby, to childhood, adolescence, maturity, old age, death, looking at the symptoms. Another is to consider the plant, looking at the development from seed to blossom as a principle of metamorphosis. The butterfly emerging from the chrysalis is a picture of the soul leaving the body at death. Waking and sleeping are related to living and dying and the idea of reincarnation and karma can be introduced in a gentle way but not as doctrine.

Before the age of ten/eleven it is not appropriate to deal with the subject of the Christ but a reverential mention of the name may be made from time to time and of course the children will know the Christmas story. At about the age of ten, acquaintance can be made with the gospels.

Between the ages of ten and fourteen, stories and talks about human destiny provide some of the right material, in particular biographies of those characters where destiny is particularly significant. Obviously, the life of Christ is included here and such personalities as Zarathustra, Moses and the apostles. Questions will arise concerning the difference between what happens accidentally in life; what may be caused; what is inherited. The opportunity will be given to deal with questions concerning life and death, reincarnation, karma, immortality. In the Bible mention is made of higher beings (hierarchies) and in this connection they can be discussed and explained (angels, etc.). The gospels can be studied and it should be pointed out that each presents a different point of view.

In the Upper School the 'tone' of the lessons has to be somewhat different. Adolescents no longer accept beautiful stories or descriptions of sublime events but need to understand. They need their questions answered even if these are not formulated. The religious mood which lives in the depths of the soul (in spite of appearances) is still to be fostered but it has to be done through the activity of the mind.

The Bible provides plenty of material, Old Testament and New. In some form or another the Christ event must always be touched upon. The teacher may find inspiration in other works, as, for example, the Parzival story. Folk religions

(Hebrew, Egyptian, Greek) are a matter for study along with world religions (Buddhism, Christianity). Finally a survey of world religions will show the unique significance of Christianity.

Celebrations of the seasonal festivals must naturally find their rightful place in the rhythm of the year.

The teacher should not be constrained in his efforts but must be free to choose his own material and approach, with the proviso, of course, that he is in accord with the principles and ideas enumerated in this treatise.

APPENDIX I

Rudolf Steiner in England

In an article written in the Anthroposophical Weekly (2nd January 1927), Frau Marie Steiner mentions Dr Steiner's pleasure in lecturing in England. She writes about the open-hearted, magnanimous way in which an audience is ready to listen and about the unlimited possibilities in speaking to people who are not buried in their own academic vanity.

Dr Steiner himself was convinced that here in this country he would also find capable and suitable collaborators to further his work.

His connections with England (and Wales) came about through various interweaving webs of destiny.

His first visit was at the invitation of the Theosophical Society. His book *Mystics of the Renaissance* had been brought to the notice of certain members of that persuasion and as a result he was asked to speak at their London Congress in July 1902 as a guest lecturer. He came again several times in the following years in the same role.

Another connection resulted from an incident in Rome. Dr Steiner gave a lecture there in 1910 and among those who attended was a young English artist who was resident in Rome at the time, Harry Collison. It was an event of great significance in the latter's life and also for the spread of

Anthroposophy in English-speaking circles. Harry Collison was well-connected, semi-aristocratic, many-sided, — a barrister, a portrait painter, an active Freemason, a man of the world with a great sense of humour. He became one of the leading figures of the Anthroposophical Society in England and also edited the early translations of Dr Steiner's books.

We now switch to Cambridge at the beginning of the First World War. Here a young undergraduate, George Kaufmann (later George Adams), had come across the book *An Outline of Occult Science* while he had been on holiday and he was fascinated by it. He happened to be acquainted with the family of Josiah Wedgwood MP and mentioned the name and work of Rudolf Steiner in the course of conversation. Mrs Wedgwood was particularly interested. When the book *The Threefold State* was published (in German) she was even more impressed. She was a woman who had always played an active part in public life and now decided on action. Jointly she and George Kaufmann wrote to the author and offered to translate it. They were invited to Dornach to discuss the matter, with the end result that the book was published in English in 1920 by George Allen and Unwin. In later editions it became *The Threefold Commonwealth*.

Through these visits, personal connections and published works Dr Steiner became better known in England and various study groups came into existence, consisting at first mainly of people seeking spiritual enlightenment and of social reformers with international ideas.

In the educational field other threads have to be followed.

A leading figure of the time among professional educationalists was Professor Millicent Mackenzie of Cardiff University. A friend of hers drew her attention to the newly-founded

Waldorf school in Stuttgart. She was so impressed that she decided to investigate and sought out its founder. She conceived the idea of introducing such an education in England and discussed the possibility with him. As a result, and at her instigation, a course of lectures was organised for English teachers to be held in Dornach during the Christmas period 1921/22. This course is published under the name of *Soul Economy and Waldorf Education*. The lectures were thrown open to others with the result that so many attended that they had to be given twice over. The principals of several English teacher training colleges were present. Also among the visitors was the head of a progressive school in Kings Langley, Miss Cross. At her suggestion Dr and Frau Steiner were invited to take part in a conference to be held in Stratford-upon-Avon in April 1922, with the title 'Dramatic Art in Education'.

The conference took place as scheduled. Dr Steiner had originally been asked to give two lectures but such was the interest aroused that he was asked for a third.

Many well-known representatives of the intellectual life of the time were present, including the poets John Masefield and John Drinkwater. It is reported that the latter showed particular interest in the guest. It is also reported that Dr Steiner went every evening to see one of the plays and that during a performance of Twelfth Night he had such a fit of laughter that he attracted the attention of the whole audience and of the actors also.

Both before and after this conference he gave lectures in London to members and friends. On 16th April he visited Miss Cross's school in Kings Langley. Somewhat later Miss Cross offered her school to be developed as a pioneer Waldorf establishment. However this school closed in the course of time but was resurrected in its present form.

Another person who had become interested in Anthroposophy was Arnold Freeman, the head of the Sheffield Educational Settlement and a member of the Fabian Society. He and Professor Mackenzie organised a conference to be held in Oxford in August 1922 with the title 'Spiritual Values in Education and Social Life.' Dr Steiner was invited to speak and was supported by teachers from the Waldorf school. Here, as at many other conferences, a few eurythmists were present who gave demonstrations.

Again, many notable people were present. There were many favourable press reports. The following, from the Manchester Guardian, is an example: "At the centre of the entire conference stands the personality and doctrine of Dr Rudolf Steiner. His lectures ... vividly describe a humane educational ideal. He has told us of teachers ... unrestricted by regulations and regimentation from outside who have developed their educational methods solely on the basis of their intimate knowledge of human nature..."

In 1923 an educational conference under the auspices of the Anthroposophical Society was organised to take place in Ilkley, Yorkshire. The train carrying members and Dr Steiner passed through Leeds where the latter expressed his horror at the social inequality and material degradation manifest in this industrial area.

The opening address was given by Margaret Macmillan, the founder of the Nursery School Movement in East London, a strong-willed, energetic idealist with whom Dr Steiner had earlier become acquainted. He had been very impressed by her achievements and she had become a great admirer of his work. (On his return journey he visited Margaret Macmillan's training centre and expressed vigorously his admiration and appreciation of her work.)

In Ilkley a group of teachers formulated the idea of starting a school. Developments were rapid. A founders' committee was formed, financial backing was promised and the first teachers selected. The eventual result was the founding of the New School in Streatham, London, later to become Michael Hall, Forest Row.

Ilkley lies in the valley of the river Aire, a Celtic word signifying strong. The town is on the side of a hill sloping up to the famous moor. On the moor are Druid circles and an ancient stone engraved with a swastika-like emblem. As always on these occasions the visitor wanted to sample the locality and at the sight of these relics he was inspired to give revelations of ancient beliefs and practices.

Immediately following this conference was a visit to Wales, where an Anthroposophical summer school was being held at Penmaenmawr. This was not concerned with education but it should be mentioned that Dr Steiner was visibly impressed and stimulated by the magnificent scenery where mountains meet the sea and Druid stone circles are to be found on the heights. Again the sight of these stimulated him to speak about past events. He also took a trip to Anglesey and historic Caernarvon. The memory and the experience obviously lived with him and he spoke about the Druids in many subsequent lectures.

On the way back to Dornach he spent the usual few days in London where he gave lectures to members and also a first medical lecture to a group of invited doctors.

In view of the imminent founding of a school, Dr Steiner was asked to give another training course in England and this took place the following year in Torquay along with another Anthroposophical summer school. The educational lectures from this course are published under the title of *The Kingdom of Childhood*.

As usual on such occasions Dr Steiner was taken to see

something of the neighbourhood — in this case an excursion through Devon and Cornwall to Tintagel was arranged. Again, a visit to an old mystery centre evoked revelations, this time concerning King Arthur and his knights, Merlin and the cosmic nature of Christ.

Although seriously ill at the time, Dr Steiner insisted that no public attention should be paid to his illness and he carried through his programme without faltering. He gave several more lectures to members in London and to doctors. The lectures on medicine proved to be an inspiration for the eventual founding of homes for children in need of special care.

In the presence of Professor Mackenzie and Margaret Macmillan he gave a last public lecture on education in London on 30th August 1924.

He died in 1925. In the years since his death there has been a tremendous development and expansion of his work the world over. As far as education in the British Isles is concerned, there are now some thirty Waldorf schools, a training college in Forest Row, Sussex, and training facilities within some schools, an extensive literature and growing interest.

This survey would not be complete without mention of the homes for backward and for maladjusted children. These are more numerous than the schools for normal children and have attained far greater recognition.

APPENDIX II

Biographical note about the author

Few people have led such an active life as Roy Wilkinson and even fewer are still as active after passing the threshold of three score and *twenty!*

Roy Wilkinson was born on 13th August 1911 in the village of Shepshed, Leicestershire. At the time his father had a small boot and shoe business but both parents had been officers in the Salvation Army. Both were social, spiritual-minded people and although they had been enthusiastic workers in the social field, they found the philosophic outlook of the Salvation Army somewhat unsatisfactory. Alice, Roy Wilkinson's mother, in particular, was a seeking, pioneering spirit. Her spiritual path led her from William Booth and the Salvation Army via various churches, Christian Science, Order of the Cross, Theosophy, eventually to Rudolf Steiner. At an early age the children (two girls and a boy) became acquainted with concepts such as reincarnation, karma, couéism, vegetarianism, vivisection, pacifism and names such as Mary Baker Eddy, Edward Carpenter, Ralph Waldo Trine, Macbeth Bain as well as the new breed of social reformers — although it is doubtful whether at the time they would have meant a great deal to them.

In a desire to have access to more spiritual nourishment

and to give the children better educational facilities, the family moved to Leicester where their father also set up in the boot and shoe business. The boy won a scholarship to the Wyggeston Grammar School which he attended for five years. His reports describe him as "sleepy" and "lacking energy."

His parents discovered a Congregational church with a scholarly, enlightened, advanced-thinking — some might say rebellious — minister. Sermons and hymn-singing were only part of the activities organised there. Roy joined the drama club, the rambling club, took part in social and cultural events (recited Shakespeare) and seems to have derived more culture from that quarter than from school. In particular he made friends with an older churchgoer, a learnéd proletarian, with whom he would wander about half the night while being instructed in the beliefs of Plato, the life of Socrates, capitalism and labour, and much besides. His shining achievement at school was to win the speech prize from among 120 of his contemporaries, aged fourteen/fifteen, with a speech on 'Falling in Love.'

One of his sisters was studying in London and came across Anthroposophy. She immediately saw the light and brought the message home. Alice was interested and invited George Kaufmann to address a few friends, thus making a first direct contact with a leading Anthroposophist.

With no reluctance on his part, since he was not particularly enamoured of the offerings of the grammar school, Roy was sent to Dornach to attend the upper classes of a Rudolf Steiner school. His parents could only make a small contribution to the fees, so it was arranged that he should work his passage by washing-up and doing various other chores.

After two years he returned to England and worked for a time with his father selling shoes in the market place but he had a yen to return to Dornach to take the speech and drama course. Financially this was an impossible burden for his parents but they were determined that he should follow his instincts, and, by a combination of their support, concessions on the part of the Goetheanum and self-effort, it became possible to do the four-year course and be rewarded with a diploma from Frau Dr Steiner.

Roy then came to England to work for a time at the Anthroposophical centre in Ilkeston. During this time he organised and conducted the first eurythmy tours in England — Ilkeston, Nottingham, Derby, Sheffield, Leicester, Manchester, Liverpool, Bradford. This was a real cultivating of the wilderness but it met with quite a measure of success and even some enthusiastic reviews. In Liverpool there was an audience of 400, in Bradford, 300 — full houses.

One of the highlights (for the artistes) was when he decided that these tender maidens ought to see something of the real world and so organised a trip for them down a coal mine. He records with some glee (and a little remorse) how the girls were persuaded to take a ride on the conveyor belt at the coal face and were deposited at the end on a heap of coal.

The ruling body at Ilkeston now wanted to put all its resources into the founding of a school and Roy was approached about becoming the first teacher. At the time however he did not feel that this was his métier and while in a state of limbo he received an invitation to join the staff of the Anthroposophical medical firm, the Weleda, in London.

Accepting the post meant having the means to get married and to live in the great city, both attractive propositions at the time. But life in London became irksome, his health suffered and he longed for the trees and the fields and the open countryside. Fate stepped in with the opportunity of working in agriculture. In many ways this was a very satisfying occupation, but fate again intervened in the form of an invitation to take over the extensive grounds at one of the schools. This in itself did not materialise but the eventual result was that he became a teacher.

A severe illness put him out of action for almost a year but having recovered from this, his real career in the educational field began. Such an illness in mid-life is a karmic matter and maybe the successful outcome meant a new lease of life and a release of that extra energy which he has since displayed.

One might look upon all past experiences as a preparation for new tasks. In Roy's case artistic activity and study of Anthroposophy undoubtedly furthered his spiritual development. Selling boots and shoes, making medicines, ploughing with a team of horses and cultivating the land have undoubtedly contributed to that down-to-earthness of his work and himself which is so characteristic.

Mindful that cities are the places where Steiner schools are most needed, he opened a school in Leeds where he worked for almost fourteen years. During this time he also had some success as a puppeteer. Inter alia he was engaged for part of this time by the corporation to give shows in the parks and squares. He also received many invitations to perform in hospitals, at private parties, etc. After one such performance he was approached by the editor of one of the big publishing companies and asked if he would consider submitting his plays — mainly based on Grimm's fairy tales — for publication. As a matter of fact little existed in the way of written texts since most were extemporised. But it was too good an opportunity to miss so he sat down, churned them out in rhymed couplets and voilà, his first book was published: *Plays for Puppets*.

During this period he was also invited to take part in the English summer conferences at the Goetheanum as chairman and lecturer, an office which he fulfilled for a number of years. This brought him into contact with people from all over the world and one result of this was a series of invitations to visit various foreign parts. In the course of time a tour became possible and he was able to take a year's trip round the world, visiting Canada, mainland U.S.A. and Hawaii, New Zealand and Australia, in the capacity of lecturer, adviser and sometimes emergency teacher. In Hawaii he was asked to make a feasibility study on the prospect of founding a school; he was the first experienced Steiner teacher to visit New Zealand and did a spell of eurythmy teaching; in Australia he was asked to write a small introductory booklet on Steiner education. This is now *Questions and Answers on Rudolf Steiner Education*. Returning home he received several invitations to teach in the U.S.A. or help found new schools there.

In his report on this trip is a little anecdote which may be of interest.

On the outward journey he had travelled to Canada on one of the old Cunarders. On the first day out he had come into contact with a group of fellow passengers who showed particular interest in his mission. Thereafter, after a bout of early morning sickness (sea-sickness) he held a daily study group on deck on Anthroposophy.

To detail all subsequent teaching activities would mean to write a book. Let it suffice to say that he taught for two years at a local county secondary school, two years at a girls' dancing school, (academic subjects, not ballet), three years at a school for maladjusted boys, a year at a Steiner school in Hamburg, another at a school on Lake Geneva and some time in Stuttgart. When a teacher of the 7th class at the largest Steiner school in England fell ill, he was asked to take over the class and he saw them through to the end of the class teacher period. Subsequently he helped in the Upper School. When a new class teacher was required he offered his services but was told that at sixty-three he was too old.

But another career developed. A year or two earlier he had written *Commonsense Schooling* and had started to write a series of educational guides for teachers. This occupation could now be followed with fresh vigour. One after another the booklets appeared, were snapped up and are now in use all over the world. One eminent personality kindly referred to them as the teacher's bible. Now in retirement he was able to accept all sorts of invitations to lecture and give courses. Thus besides the world tour and activities in Britain he has, in recent years, visited Argentina, Uruguay, Brazil, Norway, Sweden, Belgium, France, Italy, Spain, Portugal, Malta.

His interest in antiquity has led him to make journeys of exploration in Israel, Egypt, Tunis and Greece.

We add a short assessment of Roy Wilkinson.

As a teacher his practicality, lively nature and sense of humour made him immensely popular with his pupils.

As a writer his style is clear and concise. Besides the series of guides for teachers, he has written several books on various aspects of Rudolf Steiner's work, and on other subjects. (See list.) His book, *The Origin and Development of Language* was published in 1992. This present work, *Rudolf Steiner on Education* was first published in 1993 and is being reprinted in his 90th year. A book on the spiritual basis of Steiner education was published in 1996 and another on Speech and Speaking in January 2000. (See book list.)

BIBLIOGRAPHY

This book is a distillation of the following works by Rudolf Steiner, for the most part printed lecture cycles or reports of his lectures. Where translations exist in English the English title is given together with the name of the publisher. The books in German are published by the Nachlaßverein, Dornach, Switzerland. The number given is the number of the volume in the Collected Works Edition (Gesamtausgabe).

34. *Die Erziehung des Kindes vom Gesichtspunkte der Geisteswissenschaft*. 1988. *The Education of the Child in the Light of Anthroposophy*, Rudolf Steiner Press, London, 1981.

293. *Allgemeine Menschenkunde als Grundlage der Pädagogik*. 1992. *The Study of Man*, Rudolf Steiner Press, London, 1990.

294. *Erziehungskunst, Methodisch-Didaktisches*. 1990. *Practical Advice to Teachers*, Rudolf Steiner Press, London, 1988.

295. *Erziehungskunst, Seminarbesprechungen und Lehrplanvorträge*. 1984. *Discussions with Teachers*, Rudolf Steiner Press, London, 1983.

296. *Die Erziehungsfrage als soziale Frage*. 1991. *Education as a Social Problem*, Rudolf Steiner Press, London, 1984.

297. *Die Waldorfschule und ihr Geist*. 1992.

298. *Rudolf Steiner in der Waldorfschule*. A collection of lectures and addresses to children, parents and teachers. 1980.

299. *Geisteswissenschaftliche Sprachbetrachtungen.* 1981.

300. *Konferenzen mit den Lehrern der Freien Waldorfschule in Stuttgart.* 1962.

301. *Die Erneuerung der pädagogisch-didaktischen Kunst durch Geisteswissenschaft.* 1991. *Renewal of Education*, Steiner Schools Fellowship, Forest Row, 1981.

302. *Menschenerkenntnis und Unterrichtsgestaltung.* 1986. *Waldorf Education for Adolescence*, Steiner Schools Fellowship, Forest Row, 1980.

302a. *Erziehung und Unterricht aus Menschenerkenntnis.* 1983. *Meditatively acquired Knowledge of Man*, Steiner Schools Fellowship, Forest Row, 1983.

303. *Die gesunde Entwickelung des Menschenwesens.* 1987. *Soul Economy and Waldorf Education*, Anthroposophic Press, New York, 1986.

304. *Erziehungs-und Unterrichtsmethoden auf anthroposophischer Grundlage.* 1979.

304a. *Anthroposophische Menschenkunde und Pädagogik.* 1979.

305. *Die geistig-seelischen Grundkräfte der Erziehungskunst.* 1991. *The Spiritual Ground of Education*, Anthroposophical Publishing Co., London, 1947.

306. *Die pädagogische Praxis vom Gesichtspunkte geisteswissenschaftlicher Menschenerkenntnis.* 1989. *The Child's Changing Consciousness and Waldorf Education*, Rudolf Steiner Press, London, 1988.

307. *Gegenwärtiges Geistesleben und Erziehung.* 1986. *A Modern Art of Education*, Rudolf Steiner Press, London, 1981.

308. *Die Methodik des Lehrens und die Lebensbedingungen des Erziehens.* 1986. *The Essentials of Education*, Rudolf Steiner Press, London, 1982.

309. *Anthroposophische Pädagogik und ihre Voraussetzungen.* 1981. *The Roots of Education*, Rudolf Steiner Press, London, 1982.

310. *Der pädagogische Wert der Menschenerkenntnis und der Kulturwert der Pädagogik.* 1989. *Human Values in Education,* Rudolf Steiner Press, London, 1971.

311. *Die Kunst des Erziehens aus dem Erfassen der Menschenwesenheit.* 1989. *The Kingdom of Childhood,* Rudolf Steiner Press, London, 1988.

FURTHER READING

Books about Rudolf Steiner education

W. Aeppli, *Rudolf Steiner and the Developing Child,* Anthroposophic Press, New York, 1988.

F. Carlgren, *Education towards Freedom,* Lanthorn Press, East Grinstead, Sussex, 1981.

S. Cooper et al, *The Children's Year,* Hawthorn Press, Stroud, 1985.

F. Edmunds, *Renewing Education — Essays on Rudolf Steiner Education,* Hawthorn Press, Stroud, 1992.

E. Gabert, *Educating the Adolescent,* Anthroposophic Press, New York, 1988.

C. von Heydebrand, *Childhood,* Anthroposophic Press, New York, 1988.

J. Smit, *Lighting Fires,* Hawthorn Press, Stroud, 1993.

B. Staley, *Between Form and Freedom,* Hawthorn Press, Stroud, 1985.

E. A. K. Stockmeyer, *Rudolf Steiner's Curriculum for Waldorf Schools,* Steiner Schools Fellowship, Forest Row, Sussex, 1991.

R. Wilkinson, *Commonsense Schooling,* Forester's Cottage, Highgate, Forest Row, E. Sussex, RH18 5BA

R. Wilkinson, *The Spiritual Basis of Steiner Education,* Rudolf Steiner Press, 51 Queen Caroline St., London, W6 9QL

Books about Rudolf Steiner

J. Hemleben. *Rudolf Steiner*, Henry Goulden, Sussex, 1975.
A. Shepherd, *Scientist of the Invisible*, Floris, Edinburgh, 1990.
R. Lissau, *Rudolf Steiner — his life, work and social initiatives*, Hawthorn Press, Stroud, 1987.

Books on Education by Roy Wilkinson

Commonsense Schooling. Account of Rudolf Steiner Education.
Questions and Answers on Rudolf Steiner Education.
The Temperaments in Education.
Miscellany. Original poems and plays, also for eurythmy.
The Spiritual Basis of Steiner Education.
Speech and Speaking in the Classroom, from Forester's Cottage, Highgate, Forest Row, E. Sussex RH18 5BA £6.50, post paid.

Educational guides by Roy Wilkinson

The Curriculum of the Rudolf Steiner School.
Teaching English.
Teaching Mathematics.
Teaching Geography.
Practical Activities. Farming, gardening, housebuilding.
The Human Being and the Animal World.
Plant Study and Geology.
Physics and Chemistry.
Nutrition, Health, Anthropology.
History. The ancient civilisations. The Middle Ages.

Other books by Roy Wilkinson

Old Testament Stories. Dr Steiner recommends that children should read the Old Testament stories for themselves after they have heard them. This collection covers all the books of the Old Testament and provides not only reading material for children but a concise

account of the contents of the Old Testament for teachers and anyone interested. It includes certain indications given by Dr Steiner
which lead to clarification of the text.

Commentary on the Old Testament Stories. The Old Testament stories
portray the spiritual development of man. They are a mixture of history and imaginative pictures. Many are only to be understood as
symbolic. This work gives an interpretation and an explanation of
the stories in the light of spiritual science.

The Interpretation of Fairy Tales. One could base a whole course of
spiritual science on the wisdom in fairy tales. Here are summaries of
some forty of the most popular stories with an explanation of the
background.

The Significance of the Norse Stories. Explanations as in 'The Interpretation of Fairy Tales'.

The Origin and Development of Language. A fascinating and instruc-
tive study. (Hawthorn Press.)

Plays for Puppets. Based on well-known fairy tales; also adaptable for
normal stage production.

Rudolf Steiner Education is based on a spiritual world view and
introductory books on this theme (Anthroposophy) by Roy
Wilkinson are:

Rudolf Steiner: Aspects of his Spiritual World View:

Volume 1: Rudolf Steiner – herald of a new age. Reincarnation and
karma. The spiritual nature of the human being. The development of human consciousness.
Volume 2: Evolution of the world and humanity. Relationships
between the living and the dead. Forces of evil. The modern
path of initiation.
Volume 3: Life between death and rebirth. The spiritual hierarchies. The philosophical approach to the spirit. The mission
of Christ.

Published by Temple Lodge Publishing, 51 Queen Caroline St., London. W6 9QT

A Lifeline

Through private donations and help from a Trust Fund, it has been possible to meet requests for some of these books (particularly the educational guides) from struggling schools which have no means of paying for them. They include schools in the following countries: Russia (Moscow, St. Petersburg, Ekaterinenburg, Voroneszh), Ukraine, Georgia, Armenia, Poland, Romania, Estonia, Latvia, Croatia, India, Nepal, South Africa.

Translations

Chinese: Commonsense Schooling. Questions and Answers on Rudolf Steiner Education. The Temperaments in Education. The Curriculum.

Korean: Rudolf Steiner on Education. The Spiritual Basis of Steiner Education.

Hungarian: Commonsense Schooling.

Greek: The Interpretation of Fairy Tales.

Spanish: Questions and Answers on Rudolf Steiner Education. (In Mexico translations of various books have been made for internal use in the schools there.)

Swedish: Human Beings and the Animal World. Plant Study. Physics. Chemistry. Anthropology. History: Ancient Civilisations to Rome, Middle Ages. The Interpretation of Fairy Tales.

Japanese: Excerpts from Teaching English. Development of Language in preparation.

Italian: The Cultivation of Thinking.

Thai: The three volumes on Anthroposophy: Rudolf Steiner – Aspects of his Spiritual World View.

The teachers' guides are in use in schools in East Europe and have been possibly translated for internal use into the respective languages.

Except where noted otherwise, these books are published and distributed by the Rudolf Steiner College Press, 9200 Fair Oaks Boulevard, Fair Oaks, California, 95628. USA. Enquiries may however be made of the author: Roy Wilkinson, Forester's Cottage, Card Hill, Highgate, Forest Row, East Sussex RHI8 5BA Great Britain.

Resources and contacts

Association of Waldorf Schools of America – AWSNA
3911 Bannister Road, Fair Oaks, CA 95628 USA
Tel: (916)961-0927 Fax: (916)961-0715
E-mail: awsna@awsna.org Website: www.awsna.org

Steiner Waldorf Schools Fellowship
Kidbrooke Park, Forest Row, Sussex, RHI8 5JA United Kingdom
Tel: (01342) 822115 Fax: (01342) 826004

If you have difficulties ordering *Rudolf Steiner on Education* from a bookshop, you can order direct from: Scottish Book Source, 137 Dundee Street, Edinburgh, EHII IBG Great Britain
Tel: (0131) 229 6800 Fax: (0131) 229 9070
E-mail: scotbook@globalnet.co.uk

or, in the USA, from
Anthroposophic Press, PO Box 799, Great Barrington, MA 01230
Tel: 800 856 5664 Fax: 800 277 7947
E-mail: service@anthropress.org Website: www.anthropress.org

For further information about Hawthorn Press books, or to obtain a catalogue, please contact: Hawthorn Press, 1 Lansdown Lane, Stroud, Gloucestershire GL5 IBJ United Kingdom
Tel: (01453) 757040 Fax: (01453) 751138
E-mail: info@hawthornpress.com
Website: www.hawthornpress.com